How Does Bilingual Psychotherapy Work? - Ideas for Interns in Training Through STORYTELLING!

by Norma Royale Wilder

PITTSBURGH, PENNSYLVANIA 15238

RoseDog Books
585 Alpha Drive, Suite 103
Pittsburgh, PA 15238
Visit our website at *www.rosedogbookstore.com*

ISBN: 979-8-88812-419-2
eISBN: 979-8-88812-919-7

How Does Bilingual Psychotherapy Work? - Ideas for Interns in Training through

STORYTELLING!

Norma Royale Wilder

ACKNOWLEDGMENT PAGE

My first book, "The Longer I Live The WILDER it gets, A Memoir of Adventure",
won the Marquis Who's Who Biographical Collection Company's 2022-23
Professional Women's Award. The biography is at the end of this book under
the title "About the Author".

Other Published Books by Norma Royale Wilder

1. The Longer I Live, the Wilder It Gets: a Memoir of Adventure
Published in Oct. of 2020

Available on Amazon

INTRODUCTION

FOR: Marriage, Family Therapist Interns, Social Worker Interns, and all other interns as well as anyone interested in this subject.

FROM the Author: Norma Royale Wilder, MFT since 1999 and a student and Intern since 1989.

RE:

This is a Resource Book, not a text book.

My idea for writing this book is to invite interns into my consulting room through storytelling to help them understand what happens there. It is completely confidential so I would never invite a person into that room but I can tell interns what happens there through this book. I have chosen these stories from actual clients and selected stories or parts of stories I thought would have teaching moments for interns. I always asked a client if I could use their story or something important that happened in the story and was never refused.

Since everything is confidential there are no pictures nor would you be able to know who I am talking about. I have changed the names for privacy.

My hope by sharing these stories is you will gain knowledge, enthusiasm, creative ideas that come up for you as you enter this most fascinating career (or calling). There are many possibilities in this field of kinds of categories where you may work over the years. Mine were mostly in Domestic Violence, Gang Kids, Sex Offenders, Teens, Couples, Families, and Multi families.

As I reviewed all the books in my bookshelves, it became clear that much of what is happening now in the last thirty years is so exciting and new, I wish I were just starting rather than celebrating my 79th birthday in August.

I hope you enjoy the stories and insights I have acquired from being in this work for thirty years. You will want to learn all you can about yourself as you learn all about your clients and how to live a healthy life personally in order to be able to give your soul to heal others.

TABLE OF CONTENTS

As I create this book with ideas for Interns in Training to be Marriage, Family Therapists or Social Workers, I have decided to separate the Storytelling from the details of the Connection of the therapist with the client which includes Talk and Emotional therapy plus introducing the Bilingual and Cultural part, Immigration and Citizenship, and Family Systems.

Chapter 1

The origin of this book evolved from a four month Spanish Supervision of three Interns in a program of a nonprofit agency helping drug and alcohol clients using Interns with Supervision. This was the first time a Spanish Supervision was offered because so many of the clients were bilingual, Spanish and English. What happened in this short period of time became evident to share in a book form as the insights and personal enlightenment were amazing. If three Interns could be so enthusiastic why not three hundred or three thousand as you prepare to work in the most fascinating career of psychotherapy. Perhaps a book would be a better way to communicate the hundreds of details that make up the use of psychology to help change lives including the richness of two (or three) different cultures.

When these three Interns had different schedules the following semester, one returning to school in the East and the other two having clients in the schools where they were assigned on the same day as the Supervision, it seemed to underscore the need for a book. Not only the Marriage, Family Therapist interns or the Social Work interns but anyone interested in doing therapy or having clients in Spanish (or any language) could find answers to this process. It might also have interest in the general public as well.

We ended the Supervision at the end of that semester. I was just finishing a manuscript for a book on another topic and the other three went their ways. During that time I came across three books that I had not seen before and thought they were superior to the list of books I had given the Interns in class. So I decided to send an email to the only Intern I had a personal email address for but included all three names. I listed the three new books and author's names and told them why I thought these were important especially as new therapists in the field. At 78 years old, I would have loved to have had this kind of information when I began studying to be a MFT at age 45. These Interns are in their twenties. How much more they have to contribute to the profession by having access to new treatment for Post Traumatic Stress Disorder and/or Emotional Incest with a nonjudgmental program.

As I said the book is a creative and fun way to have more people learn about doing psychotherapy, doing it in a different language for the client or the therapist, and understanding cultural issues as well as how people change with the intervention of Talk and Emotional Therapy.

First I will come up with a working table of contents. For example, it became apparent in the beginning that all three Interns were not sure they had enough knowledge of the language to actually do therapy as the therapist in Spanish. I was surprised because all three of them were

'Latinas' with different levels of ability in Spanish. I had done this work in two other agencies when I was working so had Interns who were Anglos, studying Spanish in high school and college. Surely these 'Latinas' had enough natural ability as all three were what I called fluent. So it was not the language that blocked them but the lack of self confidence. As we began to practice, one person as the therapist and another as the client, and using situations they currently had with their clients, it became apparent they were more than qualified. They just needed to talk with simple ordinary vocabulary to ask current questions of the client's problems and emotional status. What a difference! A simple "how do you feel about talking with me today?" or "Are you able to tell me what I can do to help you solve your problems?" are empowering the client to express him or herself using basic Spanish. What a surprise! Before long in our supervision, the three were able to relax, take as much time as needed to form a sentence or question, and not worry about making a mistake.

They had two large goals to conquer - asking the right question and doing so in a foreign language. All of a sudden the actually doing of both at the same time which had been thought daunting, became rather not so hard at all. They asked me to correct the Spanish immediately but wait to tell them what else they could have asked to better capture the problem. I tried to allow them creative space both with the language as well as their goal with the client. We even did some role playing of a difficult or defying teenager full of anger or the opposite, silence. How does a therapist deal with such spontaneous behavior? With thirty years of experience, I would tell them some of the stories that happened to me which broadened their choices of how to proceed. I also told them how I had loved the way my supervisor wove several topics like braids and tried to use her same approach. It did not work mainly because it wasn't mine. Just thinking that we each need to find our own voice and our own way to do our therapy is huge. Thank goodness these three were able to address such an important part of this learning process at such a beginning stage.

Some of the questions they began to ponder were:

1. Do I want to spend some time in the schools, either elementary or high school, until I feel well equipped to tackle more difficult populations or jump in and learn to swim while working, for example, with gang kids?
2. Do I want to concentrate on minors or deal with adults?
3. Do I want to pick a challenge like drugs and alcohol, or domestic violence, or sex offenders?
4. Do I want to work with any of these groups but include family therapy, couples therapy, and groups in therapy?
5. Shall I wait a few years before tackling the most popular therapy among therapists - multiple family therapy (minimum of three families in a group)?

So much to consider. In my thirty years of working at the county department of mental health and non profit agencies, I have done all of the above. I also had private clients including the children of the women in my domestic violence groups who grew up to be teenagers and joined my teen groups and later got married and became parents so came back with or without the partner to do parenting groups and/or parenting couples.

Here is a partial list of the categories from my experience:

1. Children
2. Teenagers

3. Adults
4. Gang kids
5. Alcohol and Drugs
6. Domestic Violence
7. Sex Offenders
8. Individuals
9. Couples
10. Groups
11. Families
12. Multifamily Groups
13. Therapy in the county jail
14. Home visits
15. Breaking of Confidentiality
16. Suicidal clients
17. Homicidal clients
18. Physically violent clients
19. Anger
20. Fear
21. Relationship with the client from the therapist's point of view
22. Relationship with the therapist from the client's point of view
23. Searching for the right therapist
24. Secrets
25. Transference
26. Countertransference

The Therapist

Let's begin with the therapist. I always tell Interns they must think of themselves first when they enter into a relationship with a client, any gender or age. Above all, be yourself, be alert, be able to move calmly from the beginning. There are rules to educate a new client that should be given before the client tells their story in the first session.

When I say be yourself, that is a big accomplishment as I have seen different ways therapists deal with clients in the office. Some work better than others. For example as a client centered therapist I always position two chairs at equal heights across from each other. A therapist who sits behind a desk or sits higher than the client might give the impression of being more important than the client or they know more. If the objective is to form a relationship with an unknown person, sitting at equal eye level across from each other makes the client feel like an equal and therefore safer.

Begin by saying you need to go over a few rules in order to protect the client. You have already established a beginning relationship by phone making an appointment day and time for the first session. Ask the person to arrive on time and clarify the directions on how to find your office. Tell the person how long the session will be, how much you charge, that you expect the person to pay before the session begins, and then ask the client if he/she has any questions so far. Asking a client to pay the session before it begins is another way to put yourself first, avoiding any problems with a client who forgot their checkbook or some other excuse at the end of the session.

When you have a client sitting down in your office who is so eager or upset they blurt out the story in a way it would be hard to stop to tell them the rules, I usually allow the person to tell part of the story and then ask them to wait until I go over the rules before continuing. I repeat the rules are to protect the client.

First, ask the client to arrive on time, have no alcohol or drugs in their system for at least twenty-four hours before the session, call to cancel twenty-four hours before the session if they are sick if possible, then say everything is confidential except four reasons you might have to break the confidentiality.

1. If the client mentions wanting to commit suicide, explain you would then stop the session and begin a crisis mode of assessing the client for information about feeling suicidal. Then ask the person about his/her support system, write down their names and addresses and telephone numbers. The confidentiality would be broken if you had to talk with the support system, the police, medical personnel, or anyone else to assure the client's safety. Tell the client you are a mandated reporter by law.

2. If the client mentions he/she wants to kill or harm another human being or damage that person's property, you would have to tell that person and the police.

3. If the client mentions they know of a child under eighteen years of age who is being abused emotionally, physically, or sexually. Explain you need as much information about the child as to his/her name, physical address, telephone number, age, race, and any other identifiers. Also ask for the caretakers names, addresses, telephone numbers, and the relationship with

the child. Tell the client you have to file a report to the Child Protective Services as well as break the confidentiality to begin finding safety for the child.

4. The client mentions an elderly person sixty-five years old or older or a disabled person of any age who is being abused emotionally, physically, sexually, or financially. Again tell the client you have to file a report with as much information that the client has to be able to organize the correct intervention.

These rules can give the client the opportunity to NOT give you any information about any of the four situations. My experience is the relationship with you may be too early to trust you but as soon as the client feels safe with you, this information will be forth coming. The likelihood of telling the therapist later is high.

I spoke to an Intern once who had a client from the same Mexican village as the Intern. The client told the Intern her family hated the Intern's family. They discussed this together and then the Intern made the decision she would have to recuse herself from having this client as a client. She told her supervisor and the client was given a new Intern. It was difficult for the Intern but she knew she had to protect herself.

I had a situation once where I lost control in the consulting room when a mother and her son began to physically fight in my office. I called for help and the family was removed from my office. We must always take care of ourselves first.

These are two different situations but there are many unexpected things that can happen. I once did assessments in a closed jail cell in the main city jail with no way to escape except to press a button for help. I was talking with an inmate when all of a sudden smoke came billowing out the vent in the ceiling filling the room rapidly. I froze from fear and was unable to press the button for help. The inmate told me to calm down as I would be OK. It was as if the inmate and I changed places - he was the therapist and I was the client. Then the smoke began to subside and finally stopped. I do not know why it happened or what made it stop. But I was glad the inmate was willing to help me. So you can see a therapist can get into situations that are difficult or make them lose control.

One final story was a girl on Probation who came into my office and refused to talk. I told her I would pick her up at her house the following week in the suburb where she lived, thinking that might help. I did pick her up and drove to the beach near by and parked with a view of the ocean. I pulled out some work I had brought and told her if she did not want to talk, I would use my time wisely to get some work done. I really did not know what else to do because I could not make her talk. I began to look through some papers when all of a sudden she burst out laughing and never stopped talking after that. So the point is we must always be calm and ready for unexpected behavior from a client, positive or negative.

The Client:

The client has probably never been to a counselor or therapist so has no idea how it works. If the therapist is respectful the chance is better for the client to be cooperative. If the client is feeling uncomfortable by the therapist, you can be sure the client is measuring how much he/ she will want to open up. The client is deciding if the therapist is going to be easy or hard to be with, whether she/he reminds the client of someone else who the client likes or dislikes, if the voice is pleasant or not, even the manner of speaking and the therapist's willingness to listen to the client and ask questions to further understand the client.

I discovered by accident how much the clients want to be not only heard but seen. I spent some of the time in the jail seeing inmates in a room divided by a thick wall of glass with a thick chicken wire made of steel on one side. It was hard enough that way to find a hole where I could see the inmate's eyes but on a day when the window was dirty, it was more difficult. We each had to move around to find the exact viewing position and then begin to talk. I do not remember any inmates who did not seek to position themselves to see me and I them. They knew I was there to help them by doing an assessment of them which would become a report sent to their judge.

In a regular consulting room there were many non verbal parts to my assessment that were not possible to observe in the jail. I wanted to observe as much as I could because it was all important information. For example, if the inmate had a tick or looked away a lot from our conversation or looked at me sideways which meant he was untrusting, those were easier to detect. An example would be a guy I talked with one day about a week after I had gone to a Cannabis Conference and learned eight to thirteen percent of all Marijuana users with no other drugs had a psychotic reaction. What? That is a lot of people and I had never come across this situation. The client became very animated and said he was a good example of this, flinging his arms in the air and demonstrating how his body moved up and down and all around when he was high on Marijuana. I knew if I had seen him in the jail I would have lost him in the small view area I had to observe him. "I kid you not, he screamed, you are looking at a looney guy who gets really crazy with just a few puffs of pot." With such new views of Marijuana use in our country moving more and more liberal, I moved more conservatively after this experience. And I met more and more of these people by asking the question which I had not asked before.

The Connection:

You may or may not have heard of a famous psychologist named Donald Winnicott who was a Pediatrician and a Psychoanalyst who lived from 1896 - 1971 and was known for two important ideas in doing therapy. The first was the respect for the mother or main caretaker for babies and young children who taught the child so many important things by playing with them, bonding in a positive way by laughing and cuddling. He believed parents needed to be "good enough" rather than perfect, not disciplining too early or too much to create a happy child who otherwise might become a false self rather than an authentic self.

The second is the connection made between the client and the intern as human beings. He even thought of the connection as a third and the most important part of a counseling session because what happened in the back and forth conversation with non verbal gestures and ways of using space together was vital to the relationship. It was different each time they came together but also had threads of former sessions in the way they developed pauses, the way they bantered back and forth or did not banter but followed repeated ways of talking from previous sessions. All of this process evolved into a togetherness that became more and more comfortable as time went on. Maybe a client asked a lot of questions that the therapist had to adjust to or ask the client to wait until a later time to ask questions. Dr. Winnicott's belief the connection as unique and mandatory for healing to happen became his 'mantra'.

Transference:

As the sessions continue a client can decide he does not like this therapist or the other extreme can 'fall in love' with the therapist. I remember this happening personally so can explain how it feels. I was at the bank and bumped into my American therapist of a few months. Because I was living in another country he stood out stronger than if I had been in the United States. So not only did he remind me of my father physically but his ability to provide a safe place in his office and be a safe person anywhere gave him an advantage that I then fantasized even more with feelings of love. I am sure this happened because the contrast of my scary assaultive father with this new man who was kind and made me feel safe and I could trust totally was such an unknown and beautiful experience for me, it did not take much to make it even more involved. The therapist was completely calm balancing reality with an appreciation for my feelings. He explained it made sense for me to interpret our new relationship as far more than it was and at the same time reality was the best part of this problem since I was not used to a father figure being so kind but I was also married with children. It was not really love, more appreciation. I am so grateful he handled this conversation in such a way I felt no rejection and agreed with him entirely.

Countertransference:

The opposite can also happen when the therapist is attracted to the client physically, sexually, or the personality of the client is attractive by itself. There are rules for therapists to follow if any of these situations arise as it is against the law to continue with the client if the therapist cannot handle the emotions he/she feels. Many a therapist has been punished for not recusing him/herself in a case of this sort. I remember attending a conference on Countertransference one weekend and was relieved that would never happen to me. The same week I had a suicidal client I was assessing for the first time and not sure what to do next. He had tried to commit suicide but failed and was now very angry with himself. I knew he was in more danger now than the first time he had tried. I excused myself and went to find the Director of the agency where I was an Intern. She came to my consulting room to talk with the client. He said he just wanted me to come home with him to protect him from himself. I was flattered and my fantasy went wild but at the same time I was grounded and knew nothing of the sort would happen on my part. I said nothing but was shocked at myself for even having those feelings. He shortly after that moved to another state for a new job. It was a good lesson for me thinking I would never have a situation like that.

Searching for a Therapist:

I always encourage an intern to 'shop around' for a therapist they feel comfortable with and then would be willing to open up to. This may not happen immediately so have a few sessions and see how you feel. It may take time and money but is always better than talking with someone you do not really feel comfortable with. It has a lot to do with the connection, the personalities, and the problem the client brings to the session. Trust yourself, always trust your emotions! In fact, this is a good place to say 'Mental Illness' is a misnomer.'! The name should be 'Emotional Illness'! I know people with PhD's who are emotionally ill. It is as if there are two systems - a mental brain and an emotional brain. I know there is not an emotional brain but to give equal rights to those two parts of our very complicated minds and body, I like to use the emotional brain as a real aspect of our mind.

Some rules of a Therapist:

I have always had a rule that if I assess a client with depression, I tell them I will not see them unless they go to a doctor, tell him of the depression, and have an assessment of what kind of depression the client has and if there are any physical reasons for the depression. My reasoning is based on the reality that a depressed person does not think like a 'normal' person thinks so it would be impossible to do therapy of any quality. The down side of this is the doctor will suggest an antidepressant or medication that is deemed helpful which brings up another problem. When I was severely depressed for several years my therapist would not allow me to take any kind of medication. His rule was medication covers up the problem he was trying to help me solve. So I did not take medication but I look back now and wonder how traumatic that was for my children to have a depressed mother for so long. I also lost a few clients who refused to go to the doctor but I knew I could not be much help to them anyway.

I had a new client once who spent the session telling me a long story of alcohol and drug use. I said very little. In the next session, the client apologized for having lied to me about everything he said the week before. He felt guilty and corrected his story. I did not know at the time he was lying. The point is 'less can be more'. I thanked him for being honest and we continued a successful relationship as a result. I remember telling my Supervisor about this and she was adamant we are therapists but not detectives, that I had not needed to go into lots of questions during that first session.

There are also therapists who have their own thoughts on how things should work and convince a client to follow their method. The therapist I liked the best was the one who did not do that. I would ask for a suggestion of how to go about changing a behavior of mine but he always would say, "if I tell you then the solution is mine and I am cheating you out of discovering what works for you". It was frustrating but now I am so glad to have known him as his way of doing therapy helped me so much more. I think it is easy to see a solution for a therapist sometimes but to give that away and not help the client discover it is unhelpful no matter how long it takes.

B. Juvenile Probation

I wrote seven pages in my first book (The Longer I Live, the Wilder It Gets: a Memoir of Adventure by Norma Royale Wilder) about working at Santa Barbara Juvenile Probation Services from 1994 to 2000. It provided an overview of the work I did there so I will now expand on that time through storytelling to give examples of how it all worked.

Juvenile Probation Services is a part of the Santa Barbara County Law Enforcement Department, a jail for juveniles that works with youth thirteen years old to seventeen years and eleven months old. There are three main Spanish speaking gangs in Santa Barbara and Goleta - the Eastside, the Westside, and Goleta 13. There are others for Anglo youth. Since I was sent there to work with the Spanish speaking gang kids, I dealt with the first three. Highway 101 separated the Eastsiders from the Westsiders in Santa Barbara and Goleta 13 was in that suburb.

There was a large juvenile facility across the highway from the Santa Barbara Jail for Adults. Next door was an office building where the Juvenile Probation Officers worked and saw the gang kids who were not in jail. It was in that building where two of us from the Department of Mental Health had our offices. It started as an experiment between the Director of SBJPS and the Dept. of Mental Health to see if having counselors at the physical facility where the jail was would help these two departments improve the communication with the teenagers in gangs.

My colleague, Karen, had the English speaking gang kids and I had the Spanish speaking. We saw the guys and girls in the jail separately, and others who lived at home but came to our building once a week to see me or their Probation Officer or came with their parents once a week for family counseling. My first goal was to get all the members on the docket to see the juvenile judge to be assessed because of deadlines for court appearances. I then did the several groups each week and then saw the incarcerated gang members later.

The first time I walked down the corridor where the juveniles were jailed, I saw a pair of eyes look at me from a high window in the door. When I approached, I realized she was a female and I burst into tears. I did not know we locked up 13 year old girls as well as boys but she was so vulnerable and young, her eyes so innocent, it was horrifying for me to see a girl behind bars. At the same time I realized my prejudice (that it was OK for boys but not girls) I knew it was also a learning lesson about life for me. It was a time to be alert to my emotions as I adjusted to an environment I had never been in before.

As I talked with these children separately I learned many unbelievable stories about their lives. Many of them had been left in Mexico and sometimes other countries while their parents crossed the border of the USA in search of work and a better life. Usually it was one parent or the other but sometimes both parents came, leaving the children with relatives or friends. This was a situation of economic necessity for the parents who knew nothing about child rearing or abandonment since they had always copied their parents and never traveled out of their towns.

For many of the children left behind, it was torture. They reported being mistreated in many ways - sexually abused, physically abused, given little or no food, neglected, thrown out into the street, verbally abused, etc. Of course this did not happen to all children left behind but for those who finally made it to the United States to their parents after months and years, many of

9

them wound up on Juvenile Probation because they had found comfort and support in a gang and then been arrested. They had joined the gangs because they did not like being in their families again after so long and after all they had gone through. In the gangs they bonded and felt respected.

So preparing an assessment for the juvenile judge, I spent time with the gang member alone, his/her parents alone, the family together, the teacher in the detention center, the juvenile doctor/psychiatrist and anyone else like a grandmother apart from the family sessions. The deadline for the court date determined how long I had for each assessment. The judge wanted to know the basics and the specifics meaning the family story plus involvement of the gang member with law enforcement, then other problems like domestic violence or drugs and alcohol on the part of the parents and the member of the gang. The judge wanted my opinion of what kind of treatment would help this family try to regain a semblance of a family willing to cooperate with each other as they had hopefully done where they came from.

I want to take a minute to say there was a lot of sameness in these cases but when I discovered a special type of situation that would be helpful to an Intern learning to be a therapist, I always asked the family or the gang member if I could use their story or something in their story that would be helpful to others WITHOUT giving any information to divulge the specific name or any information to let on who these people were. I do not remember anyone turning me down. The following stories will give examples of what I collected.

Early on I had a fifteen year old Mexican client I will call Diego who weighed 200 pounds, a tall and big fellow who was known for his anger. I even watched the Juvenile Probation Officers take a step back when they saw him coming down the hall to my office. In other words, they gave him more space than most in case he needed it to avoid trouble. But I could barely get my office door closed when this same large guy burst into tears, in terrible emotional pain over what his mother had done that week to send him into depression. She had left her four young boys with her parents and gone to another town in California with her new boyfriend to start another family. He was devastated. His being a member of a gang was the only support he had or felt he had. I saw him for a couple of years until he got into drugs and began robbing stores to support his habit. This case will return in a few years as he worked his way into my life again after becoming a Heroin addict and arrested as an adult.

Another client came to see me with his mother. Every other word was an expletive and he knew many. I sincerely did not know what to do but did not want to reward him by cancelling the session. His mother bawled him out as he continued. Then I made another appointment for the next week while I tried to think of something I could do differently. When he arrived with his mother, I told him I had been trying to follow his story the week before but the expletives got in my way and distracted me. I told him I thought he was telling me something important and could he try again this week. He repeated what he said without one expletive. He was explaining how he and his gang buddies would go out at night to paint graffiti on the side of Highway 101 except they could not run across the four lanes at once with so much traffic so they hid in the bushes on the medium between the lanes. I don't know why he wanted to tell me this story but I thought it was interesting information for law enforcement so I asked him to tell his Probation Officer. And he did. I could not tell anyone since my sessions are all Confidential. The point is I never knew what would work, what not, but just forged ahead. In this story both the expletives stopping and the client telling his Probation Officer the story he told me made major progress.

As I developed different ways to helping these kids, one of my solutions was a 'change only an inch theory'. You are aware of the saying if you repeat something over and over but expect a different solution, that is insanity. You have heard the term "baby steps". So this idea came from those. Whether it was a guy who hit his girlfriend or a wife who threw things at her husband, this solution had great results. When I told a male gang member he would have tremendous problems if he continued hitting his girlfriend so just move an inch and see what happens. The next week he came back to my office with a big cast on his shoulder and his arm in the air. What happened?! He said he did exactly what I said but in moving from her an inch he hit the telephone pole and broke his shoulder. Did he learn his lesson! And the wife who threw things at her husband reported she threw a plate sideways but at the last minute moved an inch so the plate went flying by her husband's ear. She felt empowered for the first time in her marriage which changed her whole way of thinking. She was in control of herself!

Three of my worst cases were gang males infuriated with their mothers. The first was an Anglo mother with four children from a marriage with a Mexican father. The mother had custody of one son and three daughters. The son Pedro got so mad at his mother she finally called the school he attended to ask for help because she was so afraid of him. They referred her to the Juvenile Probation Department. A Probation Officer went to her house and talked with both the mother and Pedro. He did not want to stay in her house another moment so the Probation Officer took him to the 'Juvi', the Juvenile Hall and then he called me.

There is a place in Santa Barbara where a teenager can be taken to get away from a bad family situation but if the teenager has already been targeted as a gang member, he/she cannot go there so must go to the Juvi. I then did an assessment on Pedro for the judge, the teenager was arraigned, we had a session in court, and the judge decided to send this gang member to live with his father in northern California.

The second case was very interesting because it involved a set of twins. One twin on Juvenile Probation was black and the other one was white but not on Probation. The black mother was very excitable and got into fights with her black son frequently. The psychiatrist in our weekly supervision meeting explained a woman can become pregnant twice within the first month of the first pregnancy. The mother said she loved the white son more than the black son because she loved his white father more than the black father. Imagine how the black probationer felt?! I did the assessment for the judge, the black teenager was arraigned, the court proceeded until the judge decided to send him to the juvenile boy's camp up in the mountains for several months which would give his mother and this child space.

The third fellow was sitting in the Juvenile Probation Director's Office with his mother and told the director he was very angry and did not want to be with his mother another moment. The director came to my office and asked me to follow him to his office. He introduced me to the mother and the gang member, Mario, and asked me to talk with him. He and the mother left the office so I began to find out the problem. Mario said if he had to be another minute with his mother he would physically assault her. I called for a PO (which is what they called the Probation Officers) but none was available so I handcuffed him to me and we went sailing to the Juvi next door. He ran and I stumbled he was in such a hurry. He stayed there a few days while I did an assessment for the judge. It was determined he would be better off living with a loving aunt in another town for a year and then see what had changed, if anything.

So each case is different involving many factors. Those male gang members sent to the Boy's Camp near town were brought to the Juvenile Probation Services building once a week for a group session with their parents. One night about eight families sat around a large room to talk about the similarities and differences in each family from the next with the goal of learning how to solve problems. At one point, a father jumped up and pointed at me that he was angry his son was not learning how to respect him and it was my fault. Shaking in my boots because I knew this man was a member of the Mexican Mafia, he threatened me he would cut off my fingers if the situation did not change soon.

When everyone left I went to my office and filed an Incident Report to my boss which reached the top administrators of the Alcohol, Drug, and Mental Health Services Department by the next morning. They were very upset and spoke with the leaders at Juvenile Probation Services as this was not acceptable behavior. They gave me several suggestions of how to protect myself but I knew if he wanted to hurt me he would. The next session the following week a Probation Officer joined us at the meeting. During the meeting the Mexican Mafia father tried to kidnap his son so the police were called to haul him off to jail. He and his son were no longer allowed to attend our weekly family sessions so there were no further incidents. But the loser was the gang member who we tried to see more frequently to make sure he was not in danger with his father when he got out of jail.

One day I got a call from the Juvenile Probation Director that three twelve year old boys who had attended a birthday party in a park over the weekend were arrested for starting a fire at a picnic. Since they were too young to go to the Juvi, they were put on house arrest with their parents. First we arranged a meeting of the three sets of parents, the three boys, the officials at Juvenile Probation Services, and me. All were Spanish speaking monolingual parents. The rules were explained that each child would see a PO once a week, I would do as many sessions at their homes as I needed to get a full picture of the family to present before the court. It was truly fascinating to find all three boys were 'holding the family pain' but in different ways. The first one told me about his parents fighting physically and how he tried to stop them. Nothing worked. The second one had been in his uncle's car sitting in the back seat when the uncle had an accident in which the young boy was injured. After he recovered the family did not mention the accident again rather than sharing the details with him so he could vent his fears and memories of the situation he experienced. The third child was being physically punished by an alcoholic father but he never told anyone until he told me. 'Holding the family pain' means they each had a painful emotional reason because of other members of the family not behaving well AND not dealing with the child as they should have. They were too young to be arraigned in court but my assessments were used by the probation officers and I was sent once a week to each home to do family therapy for several months. There were no further incidents. I suggested the mother in the domestic violence family go to CALM for help and all three families to CALM for a parenting class, and the alcoholic father to treatment.

Many of these teens had huge anger issues. I remember the first time I disclosed to one of them that I too had had an explosive anger issue when younger. The gang member was horrified I would share that fact with him but said he learned a lot that I did. A therapist has to be very careful when to disclose something about themselves and it should only be done after the therapist observes the situation and feels it would work on this particular client. As a person who has done my own therapy, I found it invaluable to me that a therapist would share such a personal story and each time it was very helpful. It happened a couple of times it did not work when I tried it with two of my gang kids from which I learned it might have worked in either of these cases but the client was not ready or able to hear it for who knows what reason.

Sometimes in this work an unexpected thing happens which has nothing to do with the gang member. One time I went to see a client, parked my car on the street, walked down a dirt road off the street, and saw the address was a very poor house on the left side with no sidewalk and the front door open. As I approached a dog inside the house did not see me or hear me until I stood in front of the door. Of course he lunged at me to protect his territory and I froze from fear. Luckily I had on a long skirt and slip underneath it so his teeth did not penetrate the skin of my knee but I was shaken by the incident. I scared him and he reacted.

A particularly strange incident happened when I went to visit a gang member and his sister at her house where her brother lived. Their mother had died a few months earlier so I was doing a session at their house that included grief therapy as well as checking on their relationship and any other problems that might be going on. The sister told me her mother died believing she could send her children a message from heaven to say she was all right. Next to the table where we were sitting was a curio cabinet full of glass windows and showing the mother's collection of cups and saucers, figurines, and favorite keepsakes. All of a sudden a cup moved up from its place on a saucer and then the saucer moved up into another space near the cup. Both danced around and then settled back down where they originally were. If I had not seen it with my own eyes, I would never have believed it. The two of them started laughing and saying that was their Mom connecting with them. I am still bedazzled.

I hope talk therapy will always be available to clients even though new therapies are being created without this standard way of doing therapy because it is so important for the person to make a relationship with the therapist which brings healing in a way other therapies do not. Learning to trust, feeling safe and comfortable are vital to a person changing life patterns as these three qualities may have been missing from the client's total experience in the past. I call it talk and emotional therapy since these two words are quite different.

One day more than ten years later from the stories I have been telling you I was working in the Adult Jail. I went to the nonviolent part of the jail called the Honor Farm where there were interview rooms. I walked into a room of about thirty inmates each dressed in a blue shirt and watching television. As I crossed the room to an interview room I heard a voice say, "Hey, Norma, it's me". I turned around but found no face I knew until one of them smiled. I knew that smile from when I first began at Juvenile Probation Services many years before. Yes, Diego, the tall huge Mexican fellow who scared everyone with his size and anger but cried in my office said, "Boy, is my grandmother going to be happy I bumped into you." I asked why? "Oh, she knows I won't talk to any counselor other than Norma". I then said I would come for him when I finished with the client I was assessing in the interview room. Then I told him he could find some help from any counselor assigned to him because he needed to vent his strong feelings. But he argued he did not feel safe or comfortable with anyone else.

We talked for awhile as he told me about being in the Adult Jail after becoming a Heroin addict. I then sent his judge a note I would be glad to have him in the Drug and Alcohol Court if he was qualified to be changed from the court he was presently in. The judge sent me a note this gang member was now arrested for robbery (to pay for the Heroin) and other stronger felonies so was no longer qualified for the Drug Court. I then got in touch with a Heroin counselor in an agency in town and set up a time and place to meet with Diego the day he was released from jail. He did not show. That was all I could do at that time.

I will tell a story that happened to a gang member that used another way to become healthy and learning to change but not with talk therapy.

This was a sixteen year old gang member who had gone to the Boy's Camp in the mountains for several months. It was not fenced but up in the hills behind Santa Barbara. I do not remember the actual reason or for how long he was to be there. Let's call him Luis and his friend Jorge. One night Luis and Jorge decided they were bored of being there and wanted out. They would leave the camp knowing they could not walk down the road to the highway because they would be caught and returned. So they went in the opposite direction, now dark and cold, but full of adventurous energy to see what they could find. They finally found a place they would sleep outside until the next day. That first day they walked a long way and came across a man growing Marijuana plants among other plants that covered the illegal ones. He was friendly and invited them to share his breakfast. He did not ask the boys who they were or where they were headed. They thanked him and continued their walk through the mountains, some days without food and others with more than they needed as they met other people camping or vacationing and always happy to share their food. This went on for days and then weeks until they ended up between Carpinteria and Ventura when they thumbed a ride from a guy in his truck. He was going to Los Angeles. Luis told him they had no money to pay for the ride so they created a plan the driver wanted to do to solve the problem. He told the boys they could steal a few things that would make up for the ride and showed them how to sneak into a vacant house or shop lift at a store or whatever he dreamed up.

Luis had relatives in LA so called an uncle who told them to come to his house and they would talk about their situation. My client was very close to his family and did not want to cause the family trouble hiding him from the law so Luis told his uncle he was glad the family would know he was alive and well but not ask for money or housing or the uncle asking where they would go if they did not stay.

They were gone for three more months, got caught and were taken to a rehabilitation place but lied about who they were or where they were from so were not sent back to their families but stayed at this place for at least two months, did the program there including counselors, including no ability to use drugs or alcohol, helping out physically working at the place to earn their way, and happy to have a steady and safe living situation after all the adventure and some negative times in the mountains. Finally they were told they had to confess to who they were or incarceration was the only other option.

When Luis returned home eventually he called to make an appointment and said he had returned to Santa Barbara and wanted to tell me all his news, I was relieved. The best part was his complete change of attitude and grateful he had survived and was clean and sober. The judge heard his story and decided this young fellow had turned himself around so except for leaving the Boy's Camp and stealing a few things to survive, and respecting his family by not depending on them to support him, the judge sent him to live at home and continue to be on Juvenile Probation, going to school, and seeing me and his Probation Officer each once a week.

I tell this story because it occurred to me it might work to organize a similar experience for any number of gang kids by taking them to Panama, for example, giving them some amount of money to survive a few days, and then leave them there, at least two guys together and let them find their way back to California and home. Just the idea that they were on their own and any luck of survival would be "on them", imagine all the things they would learn about themselves and their environment, what worked and what did not work in their choices daily, hourly, etc. to find food, find transportation north, hear different kinds of Spanish which they already spoke, and treat people well if they needed help or treat people aggressively if they needed to defend themselves. Obviously it would include legal permission from the parents since these are underaged teens but I bet there would be parents fed up with their child's juvenile behavior that got them on Probation and might agree to see their child given this kind of adventure to help change his attitude and learn a lot about himself. Or for some (English speaking) this might work better to have this happen in the United States but the basic idea remains for me an option that should be considered.

One of the most interesting stories while I was working with gang members happened to one of my clients and his family. It gives the reader a really good example about 'energy' and how it can change on a dime. This probationer, I'll call him Sebastian, lived with his mother and father and two siblings and the parents did a lot of fighting. The mother found a man she liked so she spent a lot of time with him and Sebastian's two younger siblings when her husband was working. One day her husband told Sebastian he had learned his wife was with this man and his other children at a public event and he needed this teenage son to go with him to find her. My client knew this was dangerous when he got into his father's car and saw his father take a gun out of the glove compartment and put it in his belt. When they got to the place, my client worried sick for his mother, his father told him to go inside the building and find his mother and bring her out to the car. When he came back to the car, he told his father she was not in the building so he got back into the car. They drove home and my client went upstairs when all of a sudden he heard a gun shot. He ran down the stairs to find his father had shot himself. The intention was to kill his wife but when that was not possible, he killed himself.

My devastated client went through a terrible time so we did a large amount of grief therapy until he could gain some normalcy back into his life after such a traumatic experience. I learned later his mother and two siblings and her boyfriend had fled to a motel to escape from her husband so they were safe. I do not remember how the father had found out where she was or how she knew she was in danger if she did not leave the event. Once I found out about this whole thing I worried what the father could have done if he thought Sebastian was covering for his mother when he returned to the car without her. Would his father have gotten angry at his son and turned the gun on him?! We will never know but thank God that did not happen.

The lesson is never knowing how quickly the energy can change on a dime according to the situation. Another similar story happened to a domestic violence family. The mother was in my women's group and the father was in a men's group with me on a different day and time. I returned to the office at 6:00 pm although the men's group did not meet until 7:30 pm. I saw Carlos, the father, at the top of the stairs sitting on a chair. I asked him why he was an hour and a half early. He said he had decided to kill his wife but as he drove to the house she was cleaning where he knew she was alone, he past by the agency where I worked and he had a group session that evening. He decided to go around the block and park near the agency and sit and wait until the group started. He said his wife would have been dead if he had not gone by the agency and found another solution to his rage. We all participated with him in session to calm his emotions and talk about what a brilliant solution he had come up with.

This group was started by me when I learned another agency that had court mandated men was more a class than therapy. So I asked my agency if I could do a group at night when nobody else was in the building and only for those men who had a wife, girlfriend, or child being seen at CALM? It was particularly impactful because none of these men had ever been in any kind of counseling except the class. I knew that being forced by the court to take the class and pay for it would not bring very good results. I charged $5.00 for two hours weekly of real psychotherapy and discovered these men all had traumatic experiences they had never told anyone way before they had wives and children. So obviously they were not normal emotionally with layers of pain that had never been treated. Carlos would have killed his wife if he had not stopped at my agency. He told us a devastating story that happened to him at age eight. He was hanging out at a local gas station with a couple of friends in his hometown in Mexico. In the back of the station was a swimming pool or reservoir. When he cornered the side of the building he saw two men throwing the other two kids in the water and laughing because they could not swim. Carlos froze and watched his two friends drown and then went and hid. He had never told anyone and carried the trauma and fear and pain inside all his life.

He stayed in the group and the other members helped me show him compassion for such a terrible trauma. He had had no ability to go get help or try to help his friends at age eight because he was frozen and scared to death if he appeared he would end up just like the others. If there is anything to learn from this it is SECRETS cause massive damage to the human heart. We will see this ongoing with these clients as well as their victims, their wives and children.

Let's transition from gang kids to domestic violence stories. I worked in several domestic violence programs in Santa Barbara where I learned a lot about the way 17 domestic violence agencies in SB work. There are shelters for women and children, groups and individual programs, family programs, multiple family programs, plus services and law enforcement to help the victims. There are court mandated classes for anger and solutions for the perpetrators as well as private programs.

I will start by talking about strange problems in doing psychotherapy with women who have experienced domestic violence. To begin with I want to make a large distinction between the two forms - domestic violence and conjugal terrorism. The second one is the less used but a more realistic view of what happens. When the word 'terrorism' began to be heard on the news coming from the Middle East in the 90's, I was surprised when the women in my domestic violence groups said 'I know what terrorism is - I experience it every night in my bedroom'. In other words their husbands came at them physically and emotionally with demands they wanted the wife to do and if she did not, the energy moved to violence. Since they had the upper hand of being bigger and stronger, the wife had to decide which way she would choose - to try and fight back or surrender to the husband's demand. Then in the same night, the husband wants sex afterwards and again she has to decide whether to keep her dignity and not fall into more demands or surrender to quiet him down. So domestic violence seems watered down and overused by comparison.

Then in my thirty years of working with these women, I was surprised they had one thing in common - a past traumatic experience that left them weak or fearful, easily picked up emotionally by the man as a woman he could manipulate. In the more than two hundred domestic violence women I worked with, only two said they had had a happy childhood. I knew both of them and their backgrounds enough to know that was not true. But besides that the man also needed to know she was strong enough to hold him up, take care of the children, take care of the home, and work outside the home to earn more money for the family.

The work was building self confidence while praising their strengths at the same time. This was all new information to these women. Each woman did individual therapy first to begin to see what they were managing emotionally before they dared to share it with a group. When they finally felt strong enough for the group, we had a rule nobody was forced to talk. So they listened to the other women who were in the group a longer time or were stronger to tell their stories. Little by little a woman became braver and braver to open up with her story and needs. It is a long process but measuring from where they started to where they arrived seemed like light years for the counselors working with them.

I am taking the time to tell you this because when we talk about domestic violence outside in the news or social groups, people say 'why doesn't the woman just leave or why do some women get into these ridiculous impossible relationships?' Perhaps this will give you a little insight into why and how this happens. There is always a precedent that holds her back - FEAR - so until she works through it and gains strength in herself, she will stay or keep choosing other men who act the same.

I will tell you a very enlightening story of just how this process moves forward. In one of my groups a mother, let's call her Maria Isabela, with children in the agency in their own groups determined by their ages to talk about their mothers and fathers fighting, was finally able to change from her individual therapy to a group therapy and then finally told the group this story. She was married and had three children under ten years of age. She and her husband began to fight more and more until one night he threw her out the back door of their house into the garden and locked the door. Her poor children were traumatized to see their mother in the garden freezing to death but there was nothing they could do for her because they were so fearful of their father. I don't remember the time sequence but I think she went back into the house the next morning after her husband left for work to get her children off for school and then found out where CALM was (which she had heard about) and went there to ask for help. She was told not to fight with her husband until she was able to take the children and go to a shelter, information she got at CALM. Now safe she got a job at a hotel cleaning rooms. Time went on, and then one day she saw a man coming out of his hotel room and leaving the building. She entered the room to clean it and discovered a woman on the bed covered with blood. My client went screaming out of the room and went home.

She told us she was ashamed of herself for not being able to help the woman but she needed to help herself first. We responded she made the right choice. A couple of years later and still at CALM learning so many helpful things and gaining self esteem, she took her children to the park one Saturday with a picnic basket. They were having a good time until a large family arrived next to them with noisy men and chattering women. One of the men grabbed a woman by her hair and beat her up, the men getting noisier and the women holding on to each other, but no-one reaching out to the woman being beat up.

When the beating stopped and everyone calmed down, my client told her children to stay at the table and then she quietly walked over to the beaten woman and asked her to follow her to the table with her children so they could talk. The woman obliged. Then Maria Isabela told her all about her own struggles and how she had found this wonderful place called CALM where she got so much help and wondered if the woman was interested? She said she was so took the name and address and telephone number and did go and got help. My client told her group she was so glad she was able to help this second time after her failure the first time. Does this give you pause when you hear people pass judgment on these women without having this information?

Another woman in that same group shared with us one night how she had survived her husband shooting her with a gun right in her stomach when she was eight months pregnant. She survived but the baby died. Just sharing that much traumatized all of us but is a very important piece of information. Some men become very insecure when their wife gets pregnant so it is the most dangerous time for the wife. Anything can go wrong and sometimes does. Another client told us her husband closed all the windows in their house and sprayed insect repellant everywhere. She thought he was trying to kill her and the fetus.

The Literature on Domestic Violence has had a statistic that has stuck in my brain since I learned about it when I was an Intern. The average times a woman goes back to her perpetrator or finds a new man who is as abusive as the last one is SEVEN. That means if a woman has only one bad husband, divorces him and finds a new boyfriend but with no domestic violence issues, then another woman will go back 14 times. One of my clients, when I told her this statistic, said, 'but I have gone back at least 40 times!!!' At her next session she said she heard my numbers and had decided she wanted me to help her get out of her bad relationship. She did and later met a very nice fellow and married him.

Juana divorced her husband and found a new guy she really liked but was afraid to get too involved so she brought him to a session with me. He asked me many questions about this new relationship as he thought she had a lot of 'quirks.' I had them both stand up as I thought I could educate him this way better than with words. I asked him to stay standing but asked her to lean over. Then I turned to him and said, 'Put your hand on her back. You don't have any domestic violence issues so go through life happy and able to have healthy relationships with women. But your new girlfriend has had difficult times of being physically, emotionally, and sexually abused, in fact she has never had a healthy relationship. That is why she is bent over.' Then I asked him to remove his hand but Juana stayed bent over. I said, 'It is as if she is still being abused as it takes a long time to learn a new way of being with a healthy partner. She will eventually stand up as straight as you but we have no idea how long that will take'. They have been married now a few years so he waited for her to change and she did. She got loved correctly, finally. She also told me her new relationship really liked how I had him stand up because he eventually saw her stand up too so it was a good visual way to explain the cure.

You can see I try different ways of helping to heal happen which the first time I do it, it is a risk. Once I was doing an individual session with a woman who kept repeating how her boyfriend had hurt her. It was if she could not talk about anything but that. I could feel myself wanting to change this scenario so I got down on my knees in front of her and apologized to her for all the things he had done to her. She immediately burst into sobs and cried for a long time and then said, 'Thank you so much for doing this. I needed this so badly.' I learned I could help where the perpetrator was never going to do it but she still needed the apology. I have used that several times, always a good healing tool.

At the end of a family session with a mother and father and a daughter and a son, they had complained about each other for an hour but as the end was nearing, there felt like a lighter side had arrived in the room so I asked them to stand up with Mom and Dad looking at each other and the two kids looking at each other (really because of their sizes). Then I asked Mom to touch Dad's nose and Dad to touch Mom's nose, then the daughter to touch her brother's nose and the brother to touch his sister's nose. They seemed a little squeamish and one of them asked why they were doing this? I said, Well, you all have been fighting for an hour but I do not think any one of you could let someone touch their nose if they were still angry. This shows me the problem has been solved. Of course they all broke out into high energy laughter.

One of my favorite ways of gaining cooperation with couples engaged in domestic violence was a Home Visit. First the female would come alone for a session with me because her husband, the perpetrator, would not step inside my office. He thought I had all the power. So I would talk to his wife and get a picture of their situation and then I would call him at home. I told him I understood his not coming because he would feel uncomfortable. I suggested I needed his side of the story to be able to help his wife so if I could come to their house and he and I could talk, it would be helpful. He always agreed. He did not feel threatened.

So I got the address and made an appointment with him. We would always have a friendly conversation and I learned a lot about him and his marriage and his attitude. When he saw I was not judgmental or on his wife's side, he usually came with her the next week for her session. From there we did couples' therapy which I always enjoyed. Why? Because all the energy is in the room. I had them sit face to face rather than looking at me so they could talk and begin to respect each other's right to talk, wait for the one talking to finish before responding, etc. This took time as respect was not a high priority for a couple having domestic violent outbursts.

I always balanced the problems of each so that each felt attended to and not left out. This happened to me personally and I remember thinking I would never make that mistake as a therapist. I felt ganged up on by the therapist and my husband at that time, two men, and I actually got up and left the room.

Unless there was a mental health problem such as Narcissism or depression, I would proceed but with depression I would have the person go to a doctor for a thorough exam for depression and a report to me of what kind of depression was diagnosed. With Narcissism, I was biased that it would never work unless the female seemed willing to try and make it work. In this case, I would proceed until nothing changed. Narcissism has many levels, we all have some, but in a case of a Narcissistic Personality Disorder, it is incurable and untreatable. I had to be careful to see at what level a person solves his problems with a total narcissistic stance. When this happened, I would inform the couple I could no longer see them as a couple but was more than willing to see them separately. Usually the man would come once but not return. The woman by now had more conscious awareness than before and was motivated to end the relationship and work on herself. There are, of course, cases when it is the woman who suffers from a Narcissistic personality disorder so the opposite happens. This is an example:

I had a private female client who came to my home and told me her husband wanted to divorce her and she did not want that and was willing to do anything to get him to stay. I told her I wanted to have a separate session with him and then see them together. To my surprise this poor Mexican construction worker turned out to be one of the most enlightened and truly consciously aware clients I ever had. He had been a taxi driver in Mexico, lived in a small town near a big city, and had a customer who lived half way between the small town and the large city. He did round trips three or four times a week and discovered the man was a psychiatrist and founder and owner of a large hospital for the mentally ill out in the country. They had long discussions in the taxi and then the doctor hired the taxi driver to work at his hospital, doing other things along with the doctor's transportation needs. After a short time the taxi driver went to live at the psychiatric hospital for six years. By the time the taxi driver got to the US, married and worked as a construction worker most of the time, he became very disillusioned with his wife and asked for a divorce. When he came alone, he told me the story of his life and positive mental health. I was able to help this family find a solution that both agreed with. She and their two daughters went to live with her brother in another city with visiting rights for the girls' father. That gave her the security of her own family with a place to live and where she could continue having a day care center where she lived so her lifestyle did not change too much. I also suggested to the father he talk with his brother-in-law about getting counseling for the two girls either at school or in the community, but separately.

When I say I enjoyed doing Couples' Therapy, it is because as much as I also like Individual Therapy, there is a limitation with only one person. They can say what ever they want so the therapist never knows if what he/she is being told is true or not. In fact the more people, the better. I also like Family Therapy, the whole family if possible, and Multifamily Therapy where several families sit in a large round space and exchange and learn how other families solve their problems. And we always started by asking the youngest member to tell the therapist what life was like at home. But if there was a grandmother present, we started with her and then the youngest. This gives the family time to relax into, at the beginning, a friendly atmosphere which usually becomes more serious and difficult as time goes by.

You can imagine everyone wants a turn to express their needs and ask questions and tell on the others unless they are afraid to. What a dynamic scene it is. As each person is hearing stories about themselves, they want to clarify or counter attack the person insulting them, etc. These family sessions can go on for a long time. The therapist has to control the amount of family talk so as to enter into the conversation with balance, suggestions for this conversation to continue at home, and then bring the session to a positive end.

One therapist can usually manage a family but it takes two therapists to manage a Multi Family group. There is just too much to watch and observe as well as listen to and give enough time to each person. Family Systems is a fascinating part of Psychology and Therapy. I will have more to say about this later and hope some of you will find conferences that deal with family systems because it will probably come up in any therapy you do.

My client, Rosario, reported becoming upset at dusk every evening. This woman was about thirty three years old, had two daughters about ten and seven, was married to a man from her village in Mexico. She had come to the agency three times before, had a different therapist each time, and always wanted to solve the problem of her reaction to feeling upset at dusk. Nobody was able to help her so she stopped after a few months and then returned later to try again. I was hoping something different would happen this time but was very surprised by what solved this problem. It was not therapy, it was not me as the therapist but her own husband who came up with the answer.

She had said from the beginning she had been sexually raped at age eight by a cousin who lived in another town. One night discussing this problem with her husband, he said, 'do you remember when you were eight years old and I lived across the street from you and one night we started kissing and fondling each other?' She jumped up, screamed, and ran out of the room. He had given her enough information that brought up reality from her unconscious! It was not her cousin who had raped her but the man she was now married to.

She got the girls and ran to a friend's house where they barricaded themselves from him and spent the night. She came to see me the next day to ask for help. First we needed to get them in a domestic violence shelter where they would be safe. Then notifying the school the girls would not be back for a few days because of domestic violence and telling her relatives and friends as well. Then getting a restraining order from the police department would legally give her boundaries that he could not get within one hundred feet of her and if he did, the police would take him to jail. She was adamant from the beginning she wanted out of the marriage as soon as possible. Her husband would be summoned to court where she would see him but he would not know where she was living. The Court now had jurisdiction over their lives as she would need money to live on if she was not working, she would need a policeman to go with her to the house to gather her belongings and the children's, too.

This can be a very dangerous time depending on the husband's reaction. They may disagree when she wants to take the beds from their house for her and the girls after they leave the shelter. Many things have to be considered and with this situation happening so fast, there were bound to be some problems. As it turned out, this client was able to get a formal divorce in a short time, sit down with her husband and a mediator and make decisions about the girls and visits and division of responsibilities, then legal issues of custody.

As for denial, this was a different kind since she had never thought of her perpetrator as being other than her cousin so the reality was in her unconscious but the moment her husband reminded her of the two of them being together but not with her permission (at age eight?), the denial changed to conscious awareness immediately.

Perhaps I should write more details about this story. When Rosario heard her husband almost confessing to raping her when she was eight years old, she reacted strongly and left her house with her two daughters. He probably knew where her best friend lived and went to find them. I had use the word 'barricaded' themselves in her friend's house which tells me I remember the details enough that he probably went there to beg them to come home. Somehow they agreed to talk the next day or she would call the police that night.

He would have been notified by a lawyer or law enforcement to appear in court within two or three days where he would see his wife but under the protection of law enforcement. He would then be accused of rape and given a restraining order not to go within 100 feet of his wife or he would go to jail. The judge would give him the day and time he should go to a meeting at a Mediator's office to talk with his wife about a new arrangement for his life situation.

THIS IS A VERY DANGEROUS TIME ALTHOUGH WHEN SHE LEFT HER HOUSE WAS MORE DANGEROUS!!! He probably obeyed the judge and was motivated to see and talk with his wife. My memory tells me he was cooperative and although not in agreement, worked out the details to visit his daughters, talked about custody issues he wanted, and generally began to realize how his new life would be. I saw his wife for several more months after everything calmed down. Her husband may have spent time in jail. I do not remember.

I want to address the issue of Restraining Orders because they are not always respected by the person issued one. I had a client taking a nap on her couch when her husband kissed her on the cheek. He had three more weeks in jail so broke the restraining order after getting out of jail early and went home. She screamed, jumped up and flew to the bathroom where she locked the door and called the police who came shortly after to take him back to jail.

Another part of this story is we always collected old telephones with chargers to give to these domestic violence victims. Sometimes one could only make one call if it was charged but this system does save lives. This last case of calling the police from the bathroom was a client of mine who had just gotten an old phone from CALM so it saved her life.

I received a call one day from a doctor in the Emergency Room of Cottage Hospital saying he had a patient that he had interviewed but found no reason for her several physical ailments so he wondered if there were an emotional reason. He had heard about the successful therapists at CALM and knew they had some who spoke Spanish. He called and was given my name.

The patient called and made an appointment. This when the therapist has to be careful as the probability there had been sexual abuse was high. It takes a while for a new client to get used to being assessed without being re-traumatized. It is imperative to NOT re-traumatize the client. Little by little the woman will begin to trust the therapist if it goes slowly.

I ended up seeing eight women over the next two years sent from the ER and all of them had been sexually abused but never told anyone. From these experiences I learned that when a person develops a physical problem, most of the time it started with an untreated emotional problem. I actually learned that fifty years ago and had seen it over and over. There is an enormous gap between therapists and doctors who are by and large not aware of this fact so it was lucky for these eight women that the doctor in the ER had this awareness and called to see if we could help. They were in the right place at the right time to solve their long hidden reality.

There are many more stories I can tell you about Domestic Violence but I want to tell you about the Sex Offender Team at CALM I was also on. After the first two years at CALM I joined this team because there was only one bilingual therapist Intern and the number of clients who needed Spanish had increased. The Santa Barbara Probation Department sent their medium level sex offenders to CALM for treatment. These were men not sent to prison but had minor inappropriate behaviors such as touching a step daughter once in a sexual way or looking into a neighbor's window watching a woman undress.

First they were assigned a bilingual therapist for individual work which included learning how to be empathic, a quality they did not have. Better said they might have empathy for their mother or other women in the family but not for the victim. Some had none at all. It is a quality we all usually learn as we grow up but these men had to learn what it was and believe they needed to use it in their lives so not to repeat the inappropriate behaviors that had gotten them in trouble. It became apparent these men had three difficult issues - lack of empathy, immaturity, and strong narcissistic traits (strong feelings of entitlement, grandiose sense of self importance, and preoccupation with Self).

After good headway had been made in the individual therapy once a week, they added going to a sex offender group once a week. The participants in the group were a mixture of offenders at different levels. The ones who had been there the longest and done the most therapeutic work could catch the rookies with their denial, game playing, and blaming others for what were their own responsibilities. After a while, the older group members graduated and the rookies became the ones to take on the new rookies. At first this was an experiment for the Probation Dept. but when there were so few re-offenders it was made the only place in Santa Barbara County where medium sex offenders did treatment.

Now you have an idea of what can happen as a psychotherapist with gang kids, domestic violence perpetrators and victims, and medium ranked sex offenders. We will revisit these themes in other chapters. Take some time to imagine yourself doing each of these groups as a bilingual psychotherapist.

The next chapter will concentrate on the relationship between the client and the therapist which I call 'Talk and Emotional Therapy'. I introduced Dr.Winnicott earlier who believed the third part of the relationship - the connection - was the most important part.

Chapter 2

A. The Connection between the Client and the Therapist is a major part of what you will be doing to ensure your experience in your consulting room is successful. You will want to learn a lot about yourself and your new role joining into a close relationship with an unknown person for hopefully a long period of time.

I was retired before I learned there was a name for my personality - An Empath. I knew I had a very sensitive makeup but the name did not appear on my radar until quite late. I got online and learned that 15 - 20 percent of the US population are HSPs - Highly Sensitive People - but two or three percent are even more sensitive and referred to as Empaths. Of those there are 8 types of Empaths. I clearly am an Intuitive Empath. This had everything to do with how I did therapy in my consulting room.

Remember you are reading about me but unless you think you might be an Empath also, you will now read about how I did my work in my consulting room but you will want to ask yourself how you picture doing this your way. There are exciting new ideas that include how to do your work and books and conferences to read and attend that will help you explore this challenge. Chapter 3 will give you information and resources that hopefully you find helpful with books and new ideas.

So, as an Empath and a Client Centered therapist, my main objective was to establish a safe and warm atmosphere, allow the person to talk about his/her person, thoughts, and emotions with no negative interpretations on my part. We would agree on rules such as the list I gave you in the Introduction and talked about in Chapter 1. I also gave each new client a list of "Norma's Ten Rules to Live Well". It actually is my treatment plan so let's take a look at it.

1. Self-esteem is everything. The lack of self esteem causes wars, divorces, domestic violence, office problems, family problems, all relational problems. Do you know how to love yourself? Do you give yourself a hug when you feel low?

   Before you can have love in your life with family, friends, husbands and wives, children, you must have love for yourself. The more love you have for yourself, the more successful you will be loving others. As we have seen in the cases of domestic violence victims, the women suffered from little to no self esteem from earlier traumas in their pasts. I would suggest that almost all the clients you will have to work with suffer from some kind of trauma, no matter what client groups you work with.

2. We all have a suffer quotient. Why? Probably the most difficult concept you will find in psychology is the idea that 'man's inhumanity to man is equaled only by man's inhumanity to himself'. I will talk more about this in chapter 3 with many book resources to help you with this most unusual idea. It's referred to as Psychic Masochism. But just look around you in the world to see both happening at the same time and everywhere. The only solution is for you to be consciously aware of yourself and then talk to your clients about this. I was always amazed how many clients 'got it' right away but some never understood the concept. So

start today and everyday by looking in the mirror each morning and asking yourself, 'How much do I want to suffer today' and then try and catch yourself as you fall into a bad thought or behavior and have the courage to change.

3. Depression is anger turned in on yourself. Really? And the extreme of depression is suicide. No kidding! And the opposite of depression is homicide. It is all about energy. And it can change on a dime like we saw with the gang guy whose father wanted to kill his wife but ended up killing himself when he could not find her. Also a person who is depressed does not think like a 'normal' person which is why when I start with a new client and find him/her depressed I send them to a doctor for a complete exam on what kind of depression the person suffers from before I can begin my work. I don't think talking about a person's childhood when he has a tumor in his body will help much, do you? So start with yourself and ask yourself what you are angry about and what can you do right now to change your energy to positive action?

4. Strive for Sweet Revenge, not revenge. To get revenge, you have to hurt yourself. You pay no price for Sweet Revenge. For example, the best revenge is a woman who suffered from domestic violence who was able to leave that marriage or relationship and was awarded in the court for the man to pay her so much a month, hopefully garnished from his earnings. Now she is free and getting money from him but no longer has to cook his meals and clean his house. Or the person who comes from a dysfunctional family and chooses to move to the other side of the country and only have contact with one or two people still in the family.

5. Equanimity (equal), not drama or gossip. May each day be calm, your energy equal all day long, no big highs or big lows. This is a hard one if you come from a dysfunctional family and have always gossiped with members of your family and/or the family lives to dive into drama five times a week. As you begin to deal with your conscious awareness you will see the need to pull back and appraise the situation. Then you can decide not to chime in and even try to ask the other members not to either.

6. The object of illusion is disillusion or disappointment. Don't create illusions but do dream and work to make your dreams come true. I just did this a month ago without awareness that the instructions on a box that guaranteed I could put the two metal rectangles in the box with boiling water and then dunk my very dirty silver pieces that had been in a box for decades and the result would be shiny bright pieces of silver thoroughly cleaned. It did not happen so I ended up being totally disillusioned. I took the pieces to a metal shop and the man said to take the pieces to Goodwill as they were not worth a nickel.

7. Each child deserves a special time, even ten minutes, a day to talk to Mama. Maybe after a story is read each night before he/she goes to bed, you might have a conversation to see how his/her day went and how he/she is feeling. It is so important because he/she may be holding information you need to know, especially if there is fear of a parent or other person in the home. You may create an ongoing time when your children may open up to you at that time of day which can help you solve problems with them as time goes by.

8. Begin talking with "I" statements when you want another person to know about you. "I feel sad when you yell at me." "I feel mad when you don't ask to borrow my things." The other person is not accused and cannot argue with you talking about yourself. This really works if you remember to do it and saves a lot of hard feelings.

9. Say three Joys a day at the end of the day and ask your children to do the same. Even when the day goes wrong, there are things to appreciate.

10. Becoming an authentic person is a life long process. What can you do today relating to others that is more real or truthful than usual?

These may seem like simple and quick pieces of good advice but they can turn into a treatment that will go on for weeks or months as each client ponders all the things that come up for them. So much of this is relational but remember to keep time for yourself in your weekly life so to be as alert as possible in your consulting room sessions. I remember my Interns were horrified the day I told them I had once gone to sleep in the middle of a session. I too was horrified when I woke up about five minutes later and the client was just staring at me, none too pleased. It was a 1:00 pm session and I was tired after eating lunch that day and not slept well the night before. All I could do was apologize.

Let me take a minute to tell you a couple of things I did to take care of myself when I had clients back to back all day. What worked for me was to take some notes while the session was going on so I had ten minutes before the next client. I finished the notes, went to the restroom when needed, and took my Japanese Metal Chime from the desk drawer and clanged it a couple of times which for me was relaxing to hear. I also made it a necessity to get out of town once every five weeks. A change of scenery was very helpful for stress levels.

All these ideas are leading up to the actual reality in my consulting time. One extremely important idea concerns physical touch. I know as a compassionate person it was easy for me to want to give a hug from time to time. But NEVER touch a client physically if you don't first say 'wanna hug?', in other words, ASK permission. They will always let you know, one way or the other. The client may have been sexually abused or physically abused or had some kind of trauma and is fearful of their space being bombarded by a well intentioned therapist. Also I remember in my own therapy being emotionally distraught one time sitting on a couch, working through the pain of my father's death which I had never done. I stayed so long sobbing the therapist got up from his chair and sat down next to me and slowly touched our shoulders. I was not upset about this but asked him later why he did that. He said my sobbing was so prolonged he thought it was a good idea for him to bring me back to reality of where I was even though he did not want to interrupt my needing to emote so long and so intensely. In other words I was in a state of childhood pain and he wanted the adult part of me to recognize where I was in the present. It is good thing to do but has to be done carefully especially if the client and therapist are of different genders.

If you are working with very poor clients who have very little money and no insurance it is easy to want to exchange a session for some service they offer. Be careful never to enter into such an agreement since it is illegal to do so. When I first arrived in Santa Barbara and started my training to be a therapist, we had an exercise to find out what the problems were among the local therapists, ethical and criminal. I remembered the main problem was charging clients with insurance more than the paying clients which not only is unethical but also against the law. In my situation I had very poor clients in the Spanish speaking community so charged $30.00 a session for thirty years, insurance or none. I had one client who was so poor he could only come twice a year, saving his dimes and nickels for six months for each session. But he was convinced he was getting the help he needed and so he came for many years.

I think I will continue by telling you about this client as he suffered from PTSD and I learned so much about PTSD that I did not know, mostly that regular therapy does not always help or not as much as for those who do not have that diagnosis. He had been a security guard and one late night was attacked from behind by a strong man who toppled him to the ground and then ran. My client had gone to several other mental health people paid for through disability but after so long without results, lost his disability insurance. He then was sent to me as a bilingual psychotherapist. Since he was a private client, my consulting room was my living room. During the winter I put a fire in the fireplace, had him sit on a settee on one side of the fire place and I sat on another settee on the other side. I always served hot tea in the winter to my private clients, and bottled water the rest of the year and in the summer used the air conditioner. This was a much better arrangement than an office with time slots, more stress for the client as well with the noise and people in an office setting, and having to adhere to other rules. I once read that Latinos are not opposed to psychotherapy, they just don't like to follow the rules and diagnosis treatment of Anglos. I always asked them to tell me the difference and how I could help them as Latinos.

One of my favorite things about working with Latinos is this: the first time we sit down to begin a treatment course and before I begin with the confidentiality rules, I feel I have received a gift from each of them as they are, as a culture, always in the moment, present time. Since as an Anglo I culturally am in the future, it is a gift to me before I can begin to hopefully help them. So I am very clear, after I give them the confidentiality rules, to have the client begin to tell me all about their life, concerns, problems they want to solve, fantasy of how it will all turn out well, and any other things they want to tell me. I might ask a question here or there but prefer to give them the opportunity to talk as much as they need to. A question might occur to me because my guidelines are truth and reality. Their reality may be different so they have to think about my question which we can discuss until I have an answer that is acceptable to both. In other words they might find in this conversation they have had a problem with the truth and sometimes that can bring the first tears coming up and we go into an emotional place. I say 'we' because as an Empath I feel their pain immediately. To be able to follow their pain, share their pain, and know when they have modified it is easy for me as an Empath. When I say 'follow' it may be with words similar to what they are saying so they know I understand. When I say 'share' I always want them to feel from me that I feel the pain they are experiencing. It is easier to communicate through emotions than through words for me and it makes them sense I am right there with them and understand. When I say 'know when they have modified their pain' I mean as time goes on and they feel better after each time they emote, I say something for them to recognize they are feeling less emotional than when they started.

A good example is a woman who suffered from her husband beating her frequently. The first time she came she brought her daughter, age 3. I as a rookie (an intern), instead of saying I could not see her with her child and we we would have to wait until the following week to continue, I sat and listened to her knowing the child was picking up the stress of her mother by her father and probably vocabulary besides the negative emotional part. I sat worried and not knowing how to handle this. She in desperation that I understand her came towards me and it felt like she was going to crawl up in my lap if I did not show some reaction to her terrible situation. That was a learning moment for me. The next week and alone with her, I was able to offer emotional support as well as words and she was calm. I knew the difference had helped her enormously.

I was aware that poor people cannot afford childcare so this woman had to bring her child. But I also knew the mother was forcing her own problems on the child. That agency where I worked did not have a childcare room with early childhood trained babysitters where the mother could have left her daughter but I think most of them now do.

Remember the story of the woman who had been in a domestic violence relationship and could not stop talking about how her partner had physically and emotionally abused her? I had no idea how to handle this situation until I finally got down in front of her to play the role of the abuser and ask her for forgiveness. She was so appreciative I did that as she felt better even though it was not the perpetrator himself. Who knew?

I had the husband of a client come in for a session so I could find out his side of the story. He was Latino from a country in South America and married to an Anglo woman. She suffered from alcohol addiction and was in a residential treatment program. They had two daughters and he worked in Los Angeles as a parking lot owner so commuted at odd hours. About forty-five minutes into the session he began to cry. I could feel the authenticity of his tears as he related stories of his childhood. He stayed in his fragile state for a long time which made me both aware of the time and his need to stay tearful until he could come out of it slowly. I had the image (which I got often with clients) of his riding down an elevator, staying on the bottom floor, then pushing the button to return when he finished. This came to me at the end as if he knew he was through crying and therefore ready to return to the present by pushing the return button. I don't know if I am explaining this well enough but I remember labeling this the 'Elevator Ride' because it happened from time to time the same way with other clients. It was different from other clients who did not seem to know they were finished crying and waited for me to ask them. All of these instances require the therapist to know when to take charge and when to wait for the client to recover.

Since I have never written or talked about these stories in this way before, I hope I am helping you understand the way the client and therapist learn to deal with each other in the consulting room. I frequently got images when I was listening to a client but did not always share my image with the client. For those times I did, I happened to be on target or the client would adjust the idea a little until he/she was satisfied that my image was correct.

Now let's talk about crying. You each will have to deal with this aspect of therapy according to how you individually are able to. All I can offer is that for most people who would go to therapy, they are holding vast amounts of pain and suffering from the past and you will not know when something so painful happens to them they have no choice but to burst out in tears. Other clients will be crying all the time and you can assess if it is better to get them into their mental brain or stay with them to discover how the crying helps them. You can make them feel comfortable crying endlessly or help them be more productive to explain and describe the pain. There are also clients who are not willing to ever open up and let the tears come. They are the ones who need to most. But like talking or not, I cannot and would never want to make them cry - in fact I would not know how. But as I sense a withholding and wanting to cry on the client's part, and if they feel safe enough, it can happen spontaneously. My experience is men are more likely to hold the tears in than women so I am likely to stop talking and let them feel their feelings and perhaps let the tears come up even though they don't actually cry.

There are three different types of tears -
1.   reflex tears which clear debris such as smoke or dust.

2. continuous tears which are 98% water.
3. emotional tears which contain stress hormones and other toxins. These are the tears that
    so need to be expressed when working with this kind of client.

When I said the therapist has to be alert how to handle, if needed, the crying of the client is
because crying for a long time releases oxytocin and endogenous opioids, otherwise known as
endorphins. Sometimes the body may become numb or feel a sense of calm. So crying is a
self-soothing action and helpful. I do not want to stop that part but it takes experience to decide
which kind of crying is happening. If I make a mistake, I can ask the client to continue crying.

In giving you my perspective on this, and after you read the most important book called, 'The
Body Keeps the Score', by Dr. Bessel van der Kolk, in which he gives many examples about
trauma but the three most difficult he describes as 'deep trauma', first children who are
traumatized by their parents or caregivers, rape, and PTSD from military service, you may agree
with me that crying is profoundly necessary in treating these clients.

And then there is laughter, not humor. Humor mostly insults or puts down someone or
something although some humor is positive. Laughter, on the other hand, is a physical reaction
that decreases stress hormones and increases immune cells and infection-fighting antibodies,
thus improving your resistance to disease. It triggers the release of endorphins, the body's
natural feel-good chemicals, which promote an overall sense of well being and temporary pain
relief. It also protects the heart by improving the function of blood vessels and increasing the
blood flow. So it is a physical not a mental exercise.

How does the Bilingual Part of Psychotherapy Interlace with the Therapy?

I felt I needed to separate the therapy and the bilingual part so to understand them better. I am aiming to help Interns who are learning Spanish as they are learning how to be a psychotherapist. It can seem that bilingual psychotherapy is extreme multitasking which sounds overwhelming but is so important to help you each find a way to enjoy doing it.

Let's start by talking about language in general. Language is the expression of how a culture or people think and feel. If everyone thought the same there would be no need to have different languages. Since there are more than 7,100 languages in the world, one can imagine how rich and different people are in thinking and feeling with words totally unknown to everyone until someone of a foreign language learns a new one. There are also many dialects, regional differences, ways of changing one language into another way of saying it.

My ex husband is from Peru. His nephews, like any other culture, speak a language they made up with their peers so their parents could not understand them. When we lived in Costa Rica one of them came to Costa Rica to spend time with us and met new friends there. He learned to understand the new language the teenagers in Costa Rica made up so their parents could not understand them. My nephew then made a tape of the Costa Rican teenage lingo and sent it to his brothers in Peru. The teenagers in Peru could not understand anything on the tape. So the variations are many, thus adding to more expression of language.

We are dealing in this book with Spanish. It is one of the easiest to learn, one of the most romantic, and according to the Internet, one of the most lasting in the future. It also has a large area of the world in which it is spoken making it a popular language to learn. Therefore we will concentrate on the details of speaking Spanish so counselors who speak English can learn the differences of this one way to communicate. You will see it is a very expressive language with many adjectives and descriptive words that we don't use as much in English.

An example of a difference would be the use of 'very'. In English we say 'he has very long legs. In Spanish they say 'he has long legs. The word 'very' is not needed. If I say I do not like apples, they say 'I do not like apple. For them, if they don't like one apple, they have no need to not like a plural of apples.

If in English we say 'I forgot the book', in Spanish it is not possible to say this. They say 'the book was forgetting to me'. Really? Is there any emotional difference because of this? From my point of view it would seem the person who forgot the book has no guilt, it is the book's fault. So there are fascinating things to learn as you discover the need for differences.

If you live in California, Arizona, New Mexico or Texas you will have ample places to study Spanish because those states provide a huge number of Spanish speaking people that feels like a language lab everywhere you go. For those of you who are in other parts of the country there are also many Language Departments in universities and colleges and community colleges as well as private schools where you can learn Spanish. Also check online courses like the one I see through emails. It has classes to sign up for or just read what they show you online each week and then find a native speaker to practice with. The cheapest way to learn Spanish is if you can find a newly arrived Spanish speaker who will exchange Spanish practice for you if you will do English practice for him/her. Now this person may not be able to explain grammar but you will have ample help with that if you follow the courses, for example:

andrew@realfastspanish.com

Real Fast Spanish
P. O. Box 533
Moorabbin VIC 3189,
Australia

You might even form a group of interns where you are in training to be a Marriage, Family Therapists or Social Workers and talk about the clients you are seeing and practice how to do therapy with them in Spanish. Watch the Spanish speaking television programs for ear practice. Then try turning off the volume and study the way their mouths move. I can talk without moving my mouth in English but speaking Spanish requires a lot of muscle movement. When I taught English as a Foreign Language in Costa Rica, the Venezuelan director would sit next to me during the classes and watch every move of my mouth which he said helped him a lot to repeat those movements as he spoke English.

I always thought it was interesting that accents are caused by vowels, not consonants. Since Spanish has one sound for the five vowels - a, e, i, o, and u - and English has many sounds for each vowel, if I wanted to say "Mister Smith" as a native speaker of Spanish, it would sound like "Mester Smeth" because the "i" has only one sound like the "e" in English.

Another way to understand that you cannot translate each word or phrase from one language to another literally was a funny thing I did with my American roommates in Spain after we went home from a year at the University of Madrid. When we wrote letters to each other we would write in English but use the Spanish form. Take the example I used earlier that it not possible to say "I forgot the book" in Spanish but rather "the book was forgetting to me". The one thing I remember we always did was say "I miss you" at the end of the letter which in Spanish is "te echo de menos" which we translated in English, "I throw you out for less". We thought it was funny but also instructive that both ways are the same in the mind of the person.

Of course one's culture is as important as the language that expresses it. My good friend, Annette Goodheart, the founder of Laughter Therapy and who is now deceased, had some very interesting ideas about culture. She loved the food, art, colors and fashions, and architecture of cultures but thought culture had a basic flaw of being so stuck in the old traditions and laws it kept the people locked into old, now unuseful ways of living that kept new ideas and practical knowledge from changing very fast.

So even though there is a not a best definition of culture, it is a system of learned and shared beliefs, language, norms, values, and symbols that groups use to identify themselves and provide a framework within which to live and work. It includes the combination of spiritual and emotional features of a particular set of people.

I would be remiss not to take a few minutes to talk about this subject. If, as an Intern, you are not doing the bilingual part, you may not come across the ethical problem of how to deal with clients already in the US, some illegally. As I said before, put yourself first and this is another area for this advice. If you are opposed to Latin Americans coming into the US illegally it would be a problem for you to work with this population. If it does not concern you, it will not be a problem.

For me it was not a problem because they were already here so I wanted to help them as much as I could. Having spent several years teaching English as a Foreign Language in Santa Barbara and doing classes for Latinos to take the Citizenship test while I was an Intern, I had a lot of information for them to go about getting some form of permission to be in this country. But now as an Intern is the time to bring this up for your consideration.

I have several stories to share with you about Latinos crossing into the US which may be of interest. The first one was a client who came with his wife and found her in dangerous circumstances at night sleeping beside her husband in the desert with other men, either crossing illegally or the 'coyotes' (the men who illegally brought them across at huge profits) who wanted to rape her. My client said he could not sleep because he had to protect her from these men. So he dug a hole in the ground about eight inches deep and the size of his wife. She then slept under him in the hole and he on top. His creative solution worked.

Another client told me that at the crossing her husband was able to cross but she was not and ended up getting raped by a 'coyote' before she was able to cross and meet up with her husband a day later.

When I was teaching English as a Foreign Language in Santa Barbara I had a class at the high school in the evening. When the semester came to a close, they decided to have a picnic in a park nearby. After eating all sorts of pot luck dishes, the men gathered separately from the women. I first joined the men and stayed for awhile until I noticed the women laughing uproariously and I was curious. I then joined their group and was delighted they would share their laughter with me. It seemed that some of them had crossed in a group and all the people in the group walked backwards to make the footprints seem like they were leaving the US instead of entering it. How creative was that?

Once they were here, some gathered in groups and isolated themselves from mixing with the dominant culture. I had clients who had been in the US for 25 years and spoke no English at all. Or the opposite happened. I saw a Latina woman one day in the grocery store parking lot get out of her car wearing shorts and tennis shoes. She was the driver. It occurred to me she had been here a long time and think of all the adjustments her husband had had to make, letting her wear shorts in public and getting a driver's license! Some Latino men would never have been able to be so flexible with their wives' freedom to adopt the dominant culture's habits.

The children would go to school, have classes in English, then go to recess outside where they gathered together and spoke Spanish, then return to the classroom for more classes in English. It was usually the women who did not work and stayed home who always spoke Spanish with their children at home. So the children went back and forth all day with each language. Other women worked outside the home and realized their children needed to speak English so did not allow them to speak Spanish at home. She and her husband could speak with each other in Spanish but the children could not understand them. Each family was different so each acculturated in a different way than the next one.

I had a Latino client who had married an American Indian and they had three children. After divorcing the man fell in love with a blue eyed blonde American woman. The man and his girlfriend and his three children and his mother lived together. So three different cultures and lots of chaos in this family. My client wanted to drop the mother of the children from being talked about but the children were adamant their mother was very important to them and part of who they were so he had to adjust to their need. The grandmother tried to give them a Latino life in the house - rules, food, etc. The new blue eyed blonde girlfriend had an even more difficult time adjusting.

One of the more interesting clients I had was a man from southern Mexico whose native tongue was an indigenous language so when he and I spoke, we were both speaking a foreign language, Spanish. Then he got a job in a church where the ministers only spoke English so after there was a lull, maybe six months, in coming for sessions he returned with a noticeable ability in English I had never heard since we only spoke Spanish. It was really different to talk in English and find him so much healthier than he had been with his PTSD because of the respect and love he gained from the ministers and church members that helped him heal much more.

I had a client for a long time married to a man who was brutally whipped and assaulted by his own father. We did many sessions alone or with her husband. They finally divorced. She married a man and moved to another town with the child she had from the first husband and then had three more children. Everything went well until she was summoned to court for being an illegal. She called me to see if I could help because the court gave her a date to be deported. This went on for a long time, the date extended several times and during that time I spoke by phone to her lawyer and even to the judge. She had never had any problems except the legal problems of her first husband. She was a regular citizen, worked full time and paid her taxes, and was distraught she would have to leave the country with her four children and the father of three of them, and even the father of the first one, so her whole family here. It was so painful to watch this. When the judge realized all the details, he dropped the deportation and ruled she could stay in the US.

Now I write about this case it reminds me of another case where a Mexican family had a five year old child so ill she was in the hospital in Santa Barbara and then taken to a hospital in Los Angeles where she died. The family was in deep grief and could not imagine why she died nor would the LA hospital explain anything to the family. It all ended up in the court and when the judge heard the mother was an illegal, he ruled she should be deported. Imagine this break up of a family in the middle of the child's death. So I went to court with her, spoke to the attorney for the family, who then asked me to speak in the court with the judge. When he understood the punishment a deportation would cause, he said if I could do family grief counseling and continue the counseling I had been doing with the mother, he would concede to dropping the deportation.

So you can see we therapists can help clients by going to court to support our clients and have better results by dealing with the legal people who make important decisions on families' lives. I even stood up in the court once when my client and her perpetrator, her husband, were seated next to each other with one interpreter talking with them. I put myself in a place the judge would have to recognize me and ask why I was standing. Furious at the insensitivity of the court, I said my client was in danger by sitting next to her husband and how could the court not have protected her better? The interpreter was asked to sit between the two people and the court continued.

The point of all these stories is to give you an idea of what happens at the border when people take a big risk or in the court how we can help them if we are willing. Think about this. I had never imagined doing any of this before I went to court but was glad I went and could help. And remember a monolingual foreigner who has never been to court is scared to death so even for just this reason I learned to go to court with my clients for support.

Family Systems

This is one of the most interesting of all categories to study as you become a psychotherapist. I will list twelve names here with one adjective to describe their orientation and a little about several of them. Then in chapter 3 I will list a few of them with important books and you can look the others up on Amazon or wherever you buy books for further investigation.

1. Alfred Adler - phenomenology
2. Gregory Bateson - systems theory
3. Murray Bowen - intergenerational
4. Milton Erickson - strategic
5. James Framo - intergenerational
6. John H. Gottman - marriage
7. Jay Haley - communications
8. Sue Johnson - emotionally focused therapy
9. Cloe Madanes - strategic
10. Salvador Minuchin - structural
11. Virginia Satir - conjoint
12. Carl Witaker - family systems

Before I continue I will add the current most popular one, Internal Family systems, which I did not have any contact with but you can find conferences, books, and other sources about this new and exciting trend in Family Therapy. The best part I read about online is that it is centered in dealing with emotions, thank heavens! It focuses on saying the undamaged part of a client is who the person is and the rest can be dealt with to strengthen the person. Sounds very needed by many people. Dr. Richard Schwartz is the main therapist who gives conferences on this subject.

The three I found the most interesting in my time were John Gottman, Salvador Minuchin, and Murray Bowen. I attended conferences and had special experiments where I was an Intern to learn more about these three. After ten years being retired and writing and publishing two books, I read Harville Hendrick's book, "Getting the Love You Want" which I have two copies of but do not remember reading it thirty years ago. It is for couples, the executive sub system of the family, and deals incredibly deep into defusing the age old 'power struggle' that couples deal with. I decided to make it one of the three most important books to read which you will see in Chapter 3.

As for enticing some of you to use your psychotherapy degree in a very useful way and any of you interested in working with Law Enforcement, consider the case of the Las Vegas shooter who shoot 58 people from his hotel room high above and overlooking a rock concert. To this day the police have never discovered the motive. For me it has a clear motive from Family Systems research. This man's father was a notorious bank robber on the Most Wanted List for many years and died killing other people along with himself. His son, with the inherited negative family energy, must have wanted to 'out shine' his Dad so since he was in failing health decided to die and have infamy on his way out. If that is not enough to convince you, his other brother who had no criminal record, started to get in trouble with the law several months after his shooter brother's death. For those who study Family systems, you might want to work with the Law.

Chapter 3

Part 1 - Your toolbox called "Three Concepts and three Books".

If you never read anymore books or wonder what the three most important ideas are in psychology in my humble estimation, read on...

My three most important books I think will help you:

1. 'The Body Keeps the Score' by Bessel van der Kolk - For the last 20 years this psychiatrist has been trying to get a new DSM entry on Trauma called 'Deep Trauma' with no success. It is the most important book I have read in my entire career and hope you do not wait another minute before you get it on Amazon. He believes the following three types of trauma - Child Abuse of any kind by the parents or caregivers, Rape, and PTSD from any military experience are the main severest traumas although there are many other kinds. I have read it several times and given it to friends and colleagues all of whom said they felt treated for their own problems by reading the book as well as informed about so much about trauma in general. He also gives conferences by Zoom. I see the conference announcements on Facebook but I am sure there are other ways to find out about them. I think I paid $18.00 for a copy.

2. 'The Emotional Incest Syndrome' by Pat Love - I hope many of you decide to study Family Systems as it will help you immensely. Not only does the author explain some of the different types of emotional incest in the first half of the book but the last half is a comprehensive way to do the therapy in a non-judgmental way. I have never seen this in the last half of a book about how to treat the content of the problem and also without judgment. I met this author twice at two conferences and enjoyed some private conversations with her. What a insightful human being.

3. 'Getting the Love You Want' by Harville Hendricks' - As I mentioned in Chapter 2, I read this recently and was astounded how important this book is. I have just added it to the most important books you will want to read. I found two copies of the book on my bookshelves but do not remember reading it thirty years ago. I do believe I would have been a much better Couples Therapist if I had used this book while working. So now you all can know how to do this important work from the beginning.

Part 2   Concepts -

Remember these are my opinions based on 30 years doing psychotherapy. You are free to develop your own beliefs as you work in this field. This is just one Marriage, Family Therapist's opinion after 2,000 clients.

1. PSYCHIC MASOCHISM - This is probably the hardest concept to understand so I want to
    give you a chance to look this person up on line after my short paragraph here. Edmund
    Bergler was born in what is now Ukraine in 1899 but later moved to Austria and then fled
    from the Nazi' to New York City in 1937. From a Jewish family and one of Freud's closest
    colleagues, he is best known for this concept and wrote 22 books about it (all on Amazon).
    He called this concept the Basic Neurosis which he defined as 'Man's inhumanity to man is
    equaled only by Man's inhumanity to himself'. He said that people were heavily defended
    against the realization of the darkest aspects of human nature, meaning the individual's
    emotional addiction to unresolved negative emotions. There have been countless
    psychologists who have studied this concept over many years, including Sigmund Freud and
    Carl Jung. My personal therapist has studied this concept for sixty years and written six
    books about it and transforms the meaning of it as "There is only one Disease - the need to
    suffer". It is quite fascinating as you can see so I hope you find your own best way to
    understand it.

2. CONSCIOUS AWARENESS - The words Human Consciousness refers to your individual
    awareness of your unique thoughts, memories, feelings, sensations, and environments.
    Essentially your consciousness is your awareness of yourself and the world around you.
    This awareness is subjective and unique to you. I formed a group of therapists who are
    my close friends and what we discovered early on was that we are the only person in our
    family of origin who sees and hears and understands the psychological problems of our
    family members. Everyone else is in denial, meaning they do not yet have an understanding
    of the others in the family. At some point maybe before or during the study to be a Marriage,
    Family therapist we all began to have insights about our families and our role in them as a
    new inner awareness sprang into existence. You may be in some level of consciousness
    yourself now studying to be a psychotherapist so you perceive I am telling you the truth. It
    will only increase and help you be able to encourage this in your clients. It grew for me for
    years and then I graduated to spiritual awareness for myself.

3. THERE IS ONLY ONE REALITY. Within the therapeutic community there are two belief
    systems. One is there are many realities depending on who you are. The other is
    there is only one reality and we each are nearer or farther from it all day long. For instance
    have you heard the idea if there is an accident in the middle of an intersection the four
    people on the four corners who witness the accident will all report something different? It
    seems they have different realities of what happened. But the truth is they have different
    opinions because they each are nearer or farther from reality at that moment. One might
    have just stepped out of a bar on the corner and is drunk in the middle of the morning. He is
    farther from reality because he is in an altered state. The lady who has two children in toe
    and reaches down to tie a shoe lace will miss the accident but hear it and look up, missing
    the details so gives an incorrect report of what happened. A third person knows the person
    responsible who goes to her church so reports the other driver was to blame. And the
    fourth person sneezes at the very second of the crash and misses the part where one car
    tries to avoid being blamed by stopping abruptly and gets out of the car and screams at all
    of the people for being so careless even though the witness knows the screamer is to
    blame. You will read this and be aware to observe all kinds of things that happen to you
    from now on as you consider which system is the truth.

Alphabetical List of Categories for Finding Books

Part 3 - Books that Have Influenced Me Over the Years

If I know the person or know something about the person, I will add information where helpful.

1.   Alcoholics -

     a. Adult Children of Alcoholics
     b. From Denial to Recovery - Lawrence Metzger
     c. In the Realm of Hungry Ghosts - Gabor Mate - current important lecturer*
        I wish to make a comment here for all of you who are interested in working with
        alcoholics. When I began as an Intern we were told that for every one person who
        seeks treatment for alcoholism, 35 people die! What an extraordinary and horrible
        number far worse than any drug addiction. That was in 1989. Who knows if that has
        changed or is the same today or worse.

2.   Brain -

     a. Man-Child - Study of the Infantilization of Man - David Jonas and Doris Klein*
        If you know about or want to learn about the brain, this is a comprehensive look
        about different parts of the brain and how they function in a person and in that
        person's life. The Paleocortex and the Neocortex are part of the Cerebrum
        but evolved as opposites in the reality of their purposes. First the Paleocortex
        was significant with smell which was very important in the beginning of man.
        Much later the Neocortex evolved into the areas of reasoning and thinking. But
        currently they are considered very different - a Paleocortex person is more human
        and has more compassion and truly wants to cooperate with people. Those
        people who are dominated by their Neocortex are viewed as those evolving into
        "machines" (talk fast, unemotional, intensely cognitive) we see in the present.
        This is one of my favorite books as it is so full of information that I sat on the edge
        of my chair and could not put it down.

3.   Children and Adolescent Psychotherapy -

     a.   The Child and Adolescent Treatment Planner - Arthur E. Jongsma, L. Mark
          Peterson, William P. McInnis
     b.   The Conspiracy Against Childhood - Eda J. LeShan*
     c.   Transactional Analysis for Moms and Dads - Muriel James
     d.   For your Own Good, Banished Knowledge, The Drama of the Gifted Child,
          and The Untouched Key - Alice Miller*
     e.   The Hurried Child - Growing Up Too Fast and Too Soon - David Elkind
     f.   Conjoint Family Therapy - Virginia Satir*
          I will put Virginia Satir under the older therapists list because she is an elder in
          this profession and deserves to be in both. She has written many books you
          can find on Amazon, twelve listed (one in Spanish).
     g.   Windows to Our children - Violet Oakland*
          I knew this famous psychotherapist because not only did she live in Santa

Barbara but she and Annette Goodheart, the founder of Laughter Therapy and a friend of mine, were friends and she introduced her to me many years ago. Violet was part of the Gestalt group of psychotherapists founded by Fritz Perls that emphasized the present to the past and was famous for the role modeling exercises that I was fortunate enough to be in once. It was a powerful way to have a family interact. She told me she wrote "Windows to Our Children" after four days on her couch with a terrible flu virus and her two children were little so climbed all over her the whole time. In her pain she studied how they all three interacted. When she felt better she wrote this book.

4.   Domestic Violence -

    a.   Educated - Tara Westover*
This is a relatively new book written by a young woman who grew up in a home with a domineering father who would not let his children go to school and was against all things about government. The physical abuse was her brother that was horrific and yet not stopped by her parents. It is well written and riveting to read. A must to read.

    b.   Violent No More - Michael Paymar
    c.   Intimate Violence - Donald Dutton (and all his books)*
    d.   No Visible Bruises - Rachel Louise Synder
    e.   Why Does He Do that? - Lundy Bancroft
    f.   Not That Bad - Roxane Gay
    g.   Coercive Control - How Men Entrap Women in Personal Life - Evan Stark

5.   Eating Disorders -

    a. Breaking Free from Compulsive Eating - Geneen Roth (and all her books)*

6.   Fear -

    a. Feel the Fear and Do It Anyway - Susan Jeffers, PhD.*
This a 'Must Buy' as you will suggest to your clients to buy this book on Amazon many times.

7.   Forgiveness -

    a. How To Make Peace with Your Past and Get on with Your Life - Dr. Sidney B. Simon and Suzanne Simon
A well written book by a couple you will want to read because this is useful.

8.   Men -

    a. Death of a Hero, Birth of the Soul - John C. Robinson, PhD.
    b. He - Understanding Masculine Psychology - Robert A. Johnson*

9.	Older but Significant Writers -

a.	The History of the Psychoanalytic Movement - Sigmund Freud (and all his books)*
b.	Psychological Reflections - Carl G. Jung (and all his books)*
c.	Basic Neurosis - Edmund Bergler (and all his books on Amazon)*
d.	Gestalt Therapy Verbatim - Frederick S. Perls, M.D.*
e.	Man's Search for Meaning - Viktor E. Frankl*
f.	Neurosis and Human Growth - Karen Horney, M.D.*
g.	The First Step to Being Loved - Virginia Satir (and all her books)*
h.	The Revolution of Hope - Toward a Humanized Technology - Erich Fromm*
i.	Midnight Musings of a Family Therapist - Carl Witaker*
j.	What Life Should Mean to You - Alfred Adler*
k.	Problem Solving Therapy - Jay Haley*
l.	The Book of the It - Georg Groddeck
m.	Insight and Responsibility - Erik H. Erickson*
n.	Psychosomatic Families - Salvador Minuchin*
o.	Psychotherapy and Process: The Fundamentals of an Existential-Humanistic Approach - James F.T. Bugental*
p.	Family Secrets - What You Don't Know CAN Hurt You - John Bradshaw*
q.	A Better Way - William E. Paer or William E.P. Fairmont (as author)*
r.	On Becoming a Person - Carl Rogers (and all his books)*

10.	"Out of Box" Readings -

a.	A NewEarth - Eckhart Tolle* -
	If you have not heard of this man, he is the most popular 'out of the box' author and lecturer all over the world. He is a contemporary spiritual teacher who believes there is a way out of suffering and into peace.
b.	Many Lives, Many Masters - Brian Weiss* (and all his books) This is a psychiatrist who practiced psychotherapy for years until he had a client who changed his thinking and his career. Totally fascinating even though what happened to him probably won't happen to you.
c.	The Seat of the Soul - Gary Zuka
d.	Edgar Cayce's Story of the Soul - W. H. Church
e.	Remarkable Healings - Shakuntala Modi, M.D.*
f.	Memories of God and Creation - Shakuntala Modi, M.D.
	This author is from India but lives in the US. Her therapy practice is hypnotizing clients to go back way before the Earth came into existence and even further back than that to discover how life began. It is truly fascinating to read her findings.

11.	Physical Health -

a.	Biotypes - Joan Arehart-Treichel
b.	Somatic Experiencing, a naturalistic and near biological approach to healing trauma by Peter Levine, Psychologist

12.   Preparing for the End of Life and Dying -

    a. On Death and Dying - Elisabeth Kubler-Ross*
    b. Being Mortal - Atul Gawande*
    c. Staring At the Sun - Overcoming the Terror of Death - Irving D. Yalom*
       I have used the wisdom of this book many times with clients suffering from this
       universal pain.
    d. At Heaven's Door -William J. Peters
       What Shared Journeys to the Afterlife teach about dying well and living better.

13.   Prosperity -

    a. Creating True Prosperity - Shakti Gawain
    b. Creating Affluence - Deepak Chopra, M.D.*
    c. Most of All They Taught Me HAPPINESS - Robert Muller
    d. The Happy Empath - Christine Rose Elle

14.   Psychology -

    a. The Science of the Art of Psychotherapy - Allan N. Schore*
        This is a thick, long and very involved reading of major growth in understanding
        how clinical use is going through a shift in working with the mind and body. I
        suggest you read only ten pages at a time with the goal of finishing the book when
        you can. That is to say, there are big words and lots to think about as you read. I
        really liked it and highly recommend it because the shift needs to happen so the
        emotions are thoroughly reviewed because sometimes emotions are left out. It
        follows the way I do therapy so I felt validated with every page. If it does not
        satisfy your keen interest then by all means wait until you have done a few years
        of working with clients and return to it then.
    b. The Theory and Practice of Group Psychotherapy - Irving D. Yalom*
        This is a must for any group work you do, written by one of the masters.
    c. Emotional Freedom and the Second Sight - Judith Orloff*
        I include both books because they are very different and both exceptional. This is
        a female psychiatrist in Los Angeles who has a large following and has a private
        practice who is an Empath and does her total consulting work with emphasis on
        treating her clients with this method. I liked her long before I discovered I, too,
        have an Empath Personality.
    d. The Road Less Traveled and People of the Lie: The Hope for Healing Human
        Evil - M. Scott Peck, M.D.*
        This is one of my favorite writers because he treats a whole spectrum of ideas.
        He was a psychiatrist who on the one hand dealt with what goes on in the
        consulting room toward maturity, mental and spiritual growth on a long journey
        of discovery and the opposite is what I said earlier about 'Psychic Masochism',
        'Man's inhumanity to man is equalled only by man's inhumanity to himself.' The
        Road Less Traveled book deals with stories of the first part. 'People of the Lie' is
        about evil. The stories are fascinating.

15.   Relationships -

a. Life Colors and Love Colors - Pamala Oslie*
This is the first psychic I went to and was amazed how accurate her assessment
of me was. I bought both her books that have exercises to find out what your
unique auras reveal. She is a truly sensitive visionary.
b. Giving the Love that Heals and Keeping the Love you Find - Harville Hendricks*
This is the author of 'Getting the Love You Want' that I listed as one of three best
books I suggested to you. All three are important but the guide for couples will
save many marriages.
c. The Seven Principles for Making Marriage Work - John M. Gottman, PhD.*
I was lucky that I got a lot of practical knowledge from this well known clinician in
my training by two professors that trained with him.
d. Men Are from Mars, Women Are from Venus - John Gray, PhD.*
This was a well known book with a fancy title but when I read it, I was surprised it
was so well written and relevant.
e. Soul Mates - Thomas Moore
f. Couple Skills - Making Your Relationship Work - Matthew McKay, PhD.
g. Birth and Relationships - Sondra Ray and Bob Mandel
h. Creative Intimacy - Dr. Jerry Greenwald
i. Uncoupling - Diane Vaughan
j. Coming Apart and Why Relationships End - Daphne Rose Kingma
k. Brothers and Sisters - How they Shape Our Lives - Jane Mersky Leder
l. Healing Your Emotional Self and the Jekyll and Hyde Syndrome - Beverly Engel*
This author lived for a couple of years in Santa Barbara and was the Director of a
Shelter for Women program. I talked to her various times during her stay and
found her fascinating.
m. Too Good to Leave, Too Bad to Stay - Mamie Williams
Only 52 pages long, this is an excellent book that answers all the questions of a
person in this dilemma.

16. Sex -

a. We're Having Sex Right Now - Dr. William E.P. Fairmont
This is a fascinating book written by a Freudian Psychologist that deals with all
information you need to know about how everything we do in life is sexual since
we were all born through sexual conception between a man and woman. But it
is so much more and written from a very unique point of view which you will find
truly unexpected.

17. Therapists -

a. The Wounded Healer - The Pain and Joy of Caregiving - Omar Reda, M.D.
I just found this book advertised in this month's Psychotherapy Networker magazine
which reminded me I had not mentioned this phenomenon. I know nothing about
this book but assume it will give us a good idea of people like you and me that
choose this line of work because we were wounded probably in childhood and feel
compelled to help others after we have recovered ourselves. My experience of
my colleagues and others I have known show three categories: One, I know many
therapists who come from healthy, happy homes. They make good role

Most of my therapeutic friends are like me, wounded in childhood which affected my life so I was drawn to want to help others. There is also a third group which I will describe as 'looking to see how they fit into the mental illness' category so have a personal reason, not what I call a compassionate reason for studying psychology. I hope the Wounded Healer is the largest group as I truly believe our experience in trauma is a vital way to connect with a client.

b. How's Your Family Really Doing? - Debra Manchester MacMannis*, M.S.W. and Don MacMannis, PhD.*
I regard Debra Manchester as the Best family therapist in Santa Barbara. I have followed her for years after she did a series of lectures on Family Therapy at CALM, attending lectures in the community she has done with her husband, and finally doing a short stint of sessions myself. I know you will find this book a resource you will use over and over.

18.   Trauma -

   a. The Body Keeps the Score - Dr. Bessel van der Kolk*
   b. Educated - Tara Westover*
   c. The Emotional Incest Syndrome - Pat Love*

19.   Violent Behavior -

   a. Violence in America - Arnold P. Goldstein
   b. Inside the Criminal Mind - Stanton E. Samenow, PhD.*
   c. The Mask of Sanity - Mosby Medical Library
   d. Psychopathy - Wiley Series on Personality Processes
   e. Snakes in Suits - Paul Bobiak and Robert Hare
   f. Without Conscience - Robert Hare*
   g. Telling Lies - Paul Ekman

20.   Women -

   a. She - Understanding Feminine Psychology - Robert A. Johnson*
   b. Women Who Run With the Wolves - Clarissa Pinkola Estes, PhD.*

21.   The Spanish Language -

   a. The Literature of the Spanish People - Gerald Brenan
   b. Correct Your Spanish Blunders - Jean Yates
   c. 2001 Spanish and English Idioms - Dr. Pablo Garcia Loaeza
   d. Workbook - Spanish Now 1 - Ruth J. Sitverstein
   e. Real Fast Spanish - current way to take classes online - email:
         andrew@realfastspanish.com

1. These are some random last ideas that you may or may not click with but I feel are more things for you to consider.

   I have never thought that 'gray' was a color. I think of it as a mood that is represented by the color 'gray'. That mood is mostly depression and it is easy to see we live in a depressed era all over the United States. Every other house is painted gray, inside and out, plus rugs and curtains, couches and overstuffed chairs, table cloths, bedspreads, clothes, and any number of other things. There are reasons for this but those who do remodels and new construction of houses talk about the beautiful gray colors on television. Gray for me is not beautiful. I want to see how long it takes to have pastels and bright colors again in our lives. So if any of you end up using your wonderful training in jobs or voluntary work that help society as a whole be healthier imagine all the good you could do. There are two guys in Detroit redoing old houses they buy cheaply in poor neighborhoods and then turn them into wonderful remodels in bright colors and outlandish designs. They appear on HGTV with a show called Bargain Blocks. I hope they will be rewarded some day for leading the return to normal happy colors.

2. With all the attention given to new ways of treating Trauma, imagine working with inmates in jails who are desperate to do counseling either in groups or as individuals. There are some jails where classes are given but this needs to be a much larger system, maybe government supported to try and change people's lives. I would like to see real psychotherapy done as these inmates have plenty of time on their hands to deal with it. And since you will be bilingual, you could do this work in Spanish. Anyone interested?

3. I have a colleague who, now retired, had a private practice for years of all Borderline Personality Disorder clients. I shied away from that kind of client as it seemed daunting for me. I much preferred Gang Kids, Domestic Violence, and Sex Offenders but many of my colleagues could not imagine why I liked these because for them it was not interesting for them to work with these populations, especially with teens. I had three teens at home for a part of my years working with teens so it seemed easier to work with teens an hour at a time than have three teenagers in my life 24/7.

4. We have an 'Elephant in the Room' if I do not mention the 'election deniers' in our country. I have no interest in talking about politics but Truth and Reality are my Mantras so I want to address this issue. It has been said there are seventy million people in the United States who suffer from Delusional Disorder. I have no way of knowing how many really have this if they were diagnosed by the DSM-5 but I know how devastating this diagnosis is. It is also difficult to diagnose because these people have normal lives except for the delusion. If they are unaware of their problem it would be difficult for them to seek help for it. Unlike a diagnosis of Schizophrenia where a person has many delusions and noticeable behavior to the public that something is wrong, the election deniers only have one delusion. How this could be done to deal with this population I do not know but if any of you are interested in this subject, you would have clients for years and do a great service to your country!

ADDENDUM

1.   Autobiography in Five Short Chapters

2.   Promises, Promises - A Child's View of Incest

3.   Seven Styles of Learning

A point of clarification ... the three items contained in the Addendum are not my own work. These are writings that I thought were pertinent to the topic of this book, but I have no idea of when I actually found them or who the writers are. So please be aware that these three items are .the work of other talented writers.

AUTOBIOGRAPHY IN FIVE SHORT CHAPTERS

1)   I WALK, DOWN THE STREET.
            THERE IS A DEEP HOLE IN THE SIDEWALK.
            I FALL IN.
            I AM LOST........I AM HOPELESS.
                IT ISN'T MY FAULT.
            IT TAKES FOREVER TO FIND MY WAY OUT.

2)   I WALK DOWN THE SAME STREET.
            THERE IS A DEEP HOLE IN THE SIDEWALK.
            I PRETEND I DON'T SEE IT.
            I FALL IN AGAIN.
      I CAN'T BELIEVE I AM IN THE SAME PLACE.
            BUT IT ISN'T MY FAULT.
      IT STILL TAKES A LONG TIME TO GET OUT.

3)   I WALK DOWN THE SAME STREET.
            THERE IS A DEEP HOLE IN THE SIDEWALK.
            I SEE IT IS THERE.
            I STILL FALL IN.......IT'S A HABIT.
                MY EYES ARE OPEN
                I KNOW WHERE I AM.
            IT IS MY FAULT.
            I GET OUT IMMEDIATELY.

4)   I WALK DOWN THE SAME STREET.
            THERE IS A DEEP HOLE IN THE SIDEWALK.
            I WALK AROUND IT.

5)   I WALK DOWN ANOTHER STREET.

PROMISES, PROMISES

A CHILD'S VIEW OF INCEST

I asked you for help
and you told me you would.
I told you the things my Dad did to me.
It was really hard for me to say all those things
but you told me to trust you
and then you made me repeat to 14 different strangers.

I asked you for privacy
and you sent two policemen
to my school in front of everyone
to quote "go down town"
for a talk in their black and white car
like I was the one being busted.

I asked you to believe me
you said that you did.
Then you connected me to a lie detector,
took me to court
where lawyers put me on trial
like I was a liar.
I can't help it if I can't remember times or dates
your questions got me confused.
My confusion got you suspicious.

I asked you for help
and you gave me a doctor
with a cold metal gadget
and cold hands.
Spread my legs and stared
just like my father.
You told me not to cry.
You said I looked fine,
good news for me you said
bad news for my case.

I asked you for your confidentiality
and you let the newspaper get my story.
What does it matter that they left out my name,
they put my father's
and our home address.

Even my best friend's mother
won't let her talk to me anymore.

I asked you for protection
and you gave me a social worker
who patted my head
and called me honey.
Mostly because she could never remember my name.
She sent me to live with strangers in another place
and in a different school.
I lost my part in a school play
and the science fair,
while he and all the others got to stay home.

Do you know what it's like
to live where there's a lock on a refrigerator?
Where you have to ask permission to use the shampoo
or you can't use the phone to call your own friends?
You get used to hearing, hi I'm your new social worker
this is your new foster sister,
dorm mother,
group home,
You tip toe around like a perpetual guest.
You don't ever get to see your own puppy grow up.

Do you know what it's like to know
more social workers than friends?

Do you know what it feels like
to be the one everyone blames
for all the trouble,
even when they were speaking to me
all thy talked about was lawyers, shrinks, fees,
whether or not they'd lose the mortgage.

Do you know what it is like
when your sisters hate you
and your bother calls you a liar.
My word against my own father's.
I'm 12 years old
he's the manager of a bank.
You say you believe me,
who cares nobody else does.

I asked you for help
and you forced my mom to choose between us,
she chose him of course.
She was scared
and had a lot to lose.
I've had a lot to lose too,
the difference is you never told me how much.

I asked you to put an end to the abuse
you put an end to my whole family.
You took away my night's of hell
and gave me days of hell instead.
You exchanged my private nightmare
for a very public one.

SEVEN STYLES OF LEARNING

	TYPE	LIKES TO	IS GOOD AT	LEARNS BEST BY
1. 2.	Linguistic Learner "the word player"	read write tell stories	memorizing names, places, dates and trivia	saying, hearing and seeing words
2.	Logical/Mathematical Learner "the Questioner"	do experiments work with numbers figure things out ask questions explore patterns and relationships	math reasoning logic problem solving	categorizing classifying working with abstract patterns/relations
3.	Spatial Learner "The Visualizer"	draw, build, design and create things daydream look at pictures/ slides watch movies play with machines	imagining things sensing changes mazes/puzzles reading maps, charts	visualizing dreaming using the Mind's eye working with colors/ pictures
4.	Musical Learner "The Music Lover"	sing, hum tunes listen to music play an instrument respond to music	picking up sounds remembering/ melodies noticing pitches/ rhythms keeping time	rhythm melody music
5	Bodily/Kinesthetic Learner "The Socializer"	move around touch and talk use body language	physical activities (sports,dance,acting) crafts	touching moving interaction with/ space processing knowledge through bodily sensations

| 6. | Interpersonal Learner "The Socializer" | have lots of friends
talk to people
join groups | understanding people
leading others
organizing
communicating
manipulating
mediating conflicts | sharing
comparing
relating
cooperating
interviewing |
| 7. | Intrapersonal Learner "The Individual" | work alone
pursue own interests | understanding self
focusing inward
   on feelings/dreams
following instincts
pursuing interests/goals
being original | working alone
individualized
self-paced
having
   ownership |

1. **VERBAL/LINGUISTIC INTELLIGENCE**

    This intelligence, which is related to words and language - written and spoken - dominates Western educational systems.

2. **LOGICAL/MATHEMATICAL INTELLIGENCE**

    Often called 'scientific thinking', this intelligence deals with inductive and deductive thinking/reasoning, numbers and the recognition of abstract patterns.

3. **VISUAL/SPACIAL INTELLIGENCE**

    This intelligence, which relies on the sense of sight and being able to visualize an object, includes the ability to create internal mental images/pictures.

4. **MUSICAL/RHYTHMIC INTELLIGENCE**

    This intelligence is based on the recognition of tonal patterns, including various environmental sounds, and on a sensitivity to rhythm and beats.

5. **BODY/KINESTHETIC INTELLIGENCE**

    This intelligence is related to physical movement and the knowings/wisdom of the body, including the brain's motor cortex, which controls bodily motion.

6. **INTERPERSONAL INTELLIGENCE**

    This intelligence operate primarily through person to person relationships and communication.

7. **INTRAPERSONAL INTELLIGENCE**

    This intelligence relates to inner states of being, self-reflection, metacognition (ie-thinking about thinking) and awareness of spiritual realities.

ABOUT THE AUTHOR

NORMA ROYALE WILDER - Retired Bilingual Psychotherapist, Teacher, Community

Development Specialist

Norma Royale Wilder was interested in learning languages when she was thirteen years old, especially Spanish. She studied this language all through high school and college. In 1970 she finished her first Master's Degree in Spanish and South American Literature at the University of Tennessee, Knoxville. For 25 years, she notably taught English and Spanish as Foreign Languages in seven countries prior to entering the field of psychology. In 1992, she earned a Master's Degree in Depth Psychology (Carl Jung) from the Pacifica Graduate Inst. in Carpinteria, California.

Ms. Wilder's community development expertise began at the age of twenty when she joined the Peace Corps and spent two years in Guatemala on a community development project, coordinated with CARE, an already established agency in Guatemala. Later she did a large voluntary project in Costa Rica for El Salvadoran and Nicaraguan refugees fleeing two wars in Central America. She regards her community development service as the focal point of her life work, which also includes teaching and psychology.

From 1989 to retirement in 2012, Ms. Wilder had two main experiences in Santa Barbara, working with gangs, domestic violence, and the courts representing the Santa Barbara County Department of Alcohol, Drugs, and Mental Health Services and a nonprofit agency called CALM (Child Abuse Listening and Mediation) as well as other nonprofit agencies. Having experienced childhood physical and emotional abuse, Ms. Wilder used psychology to heal, and later pledged to spend her life helping others with similar problems. Her motto is "One person can make a difference," and her mantra is "Help the underdog".

In 2020 , Ms. Wilder published her first book, titled "The Longer I Live, the Wilder It Gets: a Memoir of Adventure", available on Amazon. It is the first of three books forming a trilogy, the other two on relationships and psychology.

I hope this book has given you some Food for Thought. I know you will read information that you will also get in your training but hopefully the peek into my consulting room offers a new perspective and gives you some ideas to help decide just how you are thinking you are qualified and interested in certain areas of treatment.

Have a simply wonderful experience as Interns to become Bilingual Psychotherapists, trying any number of fields in the vast amount of ways to do community service that brings a satisfied life to you as well as your family and nation.

9 798888 124192